Julia V. Ferguson

250

Enjoying the Art of
CANADIAN
COOKING

Enjoying the Art of
CANADIAN COOKING

Mme. Jehane Benoit

PAGURIAN PRESS LIMITED
TORONTO

Printed and Bound in Canada

Library of Congress Catalog Card No. 74-79601
ISBN 0-919364-75-6

Distributed in the United States by

Arco Publishing Company, Inc.
219 Park Avenue South, New York, N.Y. 10003

Arco Book Ordering Number: 3512

CONTENTS

INTRODUCTION

I am convinced that good cooking is an art and a form of magic. This cookbook is an attempt on my part to translate traditional Canadian cuisine into both art and magic. Over the years I have collected and concocted recipes which have been a source of delight both to my family and to me, and which I share here with you.

Canada is an enormous country with an interesting mixture of people. Traditionally, of course, there is the French and English influence; but there are other, truly Canadian, recipes stemming from the many ethnic groups who have settled here. They, together with the French and English, have given to Canadian cuisine its very special flavor.

Our food has always had a reputation for wholesomeness and freshness and, being fortunate enough to have close at hand an abundance of the best raw materials for practically any recipe, we have no excuse not to approach the art of cooking with anything less than enthusiasm and pleasure. Remembering that we are part of a proud tradition, we must continue to live up to it and to our reputation for setting a "bonne table."

Food is basic to human existence. Now that we have brought its preparation to the level of art, let us also enjoy preparing it.

Bon appetit!

Jehane Benoit

CHAPTER 1

APPETIZERS

What is an Appetizer?

In the Victorian era they were savory trifles served with sherry before dinner. Later they came under the influence of French hors d'oeuvres and became more elaborate. Today we keep them simple, yet alluring to the eye and to the stomach. We serve them as hors d'oeuvres at the table and as appetizers before the meal.

I shall give you a variety that can be served either before dinner, as snacks, after a theater or concert, or as the principal reason for a party.

The basic rules for both hors d'oeuvres and appetizers is to keep a keen eye out for contrasts in color, texture, design and seasoning.

CRUDITÉS

Let's start with *crudités*, as the French call them, or crisp raw vegetables tastefully arranged and served as is or with a dip.

Clean the vegetables. Cut as indicated below, prepare them a few hours before serving, place in a bowl of ice-cold water, and keep refrigerated. I prefer to store the cut vegetables in a bowl topped with a thick layer of ice cubes and to refrigerate them for 8 to 12 hours. They become crisp, cool, and crunchy.

Broccoli	– head only, broken in tiny flowerets
Carrots	– slivers or iced curls
Cauliflower	– tiny flowerets
Celery	– slivers or long slim fingers
Cucumbers	– peeled long fingers
Green onions	– small ones, with an inch of green at the ends
Green peppers	– thick lengthwise strips
Mushrooms	– thick slices rubbed in lemon
Radishes	– lengthwise quarters
Snow peas	– whole and well crisped
Tomatoes	– cherry type, whole
Turnips	– long thin slivers
Zucchini	– small, thick, unpeeled slices

DEVILLED ALMONDS

In the winter, guests love to eat these straight from the pan with their fingers. In the summer, let them cool first.

> **4 tbsp. butter**
> **1 – 1½ cups blanched almonds**
> **1 tbsp. each, chutney sauce, brown sugar, and Worcestershire sauce**
> **½ tsp. each, curry powder and turmeric**
> **¼ tsp. salt**
> **pinch of cayenne**

Melt the butter in a 300° frying pan and brown nuts, one layer deep, stirring and tossing often. Blend remaining ingredients, add, and stir with nuts until sugar has melted. Serves 6-8.

BLUE CHEESE CROCK

A crock is usually a cheese blended with herbs and brandy, to be spread on crisp bread or biscuits.

> **¼ lb. blue cheese (Danish, Italian, or French)**
> **½ cup soft butter**
> **1 small clove garlic, crushed**
> **1 tbsp. parsley, finely chopped**
> **2 green onions, finely chopped**
> **3 tbsp. brandy**

Have the cheese and butter at room temperature. Place in a bowl, add the remaining ingredients and blend thoroughly by hand or with an electric mixer. Pack into a small earthenware or porcelain jar. Cover and refrigerate.

The mixture may also be shaped into a roll and dipped in toasted sesame seeds, chopped walnuts, or parsley.

FRENCH CHEESE CROCK

Prepare 18 to 20 days in advance and keep in your refrigerator. Serve with fancy crackers.

> **½ lb. medium or old cheddar cheese**
> **4 oz. cream cheese**
> **¼ cup port wine, or beer, or dry sherry**
> **2 tsp. German or horseradish mustard**
> **1 tbsp. fresh lemon juice**
> **grated rind of 1 lemon**

Grate the cheese into a bowl, add the cream cheese, port wine, beer or sherry, German or horseradish mustard, lemon juice and rind. Beat together with an electric or rotary beater until smooth and creamy.

Pour into an attractive crock. Cover and refrigerate until ready to use.

CHEESE PASTRIES

Blend, chill, bake, cool, wrap, and freeze. To serve, place frozen on a baking sheet and heat in a 375°F. oven.

Cream ¼ lb. butter with ¼ lb. soft yellow cheese. Add 1 cup of all-purpose flour. Shape into an oblong roll. Wrap in wax paper. Chill overnight. Slice thinly. Bake on cookie sheet in preheated 350°F. oven for 8 minutes or until golden brown around the edges.

BLUE CHEESE ROLL

As this will keep 3-4 weeks, have it handy for emergency appetizers or cocktail tidbits.

**½ lb. Roquefort or Danish blue
cheese
8-oz. pkg. cream cheese
3 tbsp. soft butter
3 tbsp. brandy
2 tbsp. minced chives or green
onions
chopped toasted almonds
round unsalted crackers**

Mash cheeses with butter, brandy, and green onions or chives. When smooth and creamy, refrigerate for one hour. Form into a cylinder 1½ inches in diameter and roll in almonds. Wrap well and refrigerate. To serve, slice thinly and place on round crackers. Yield: 2½ – 3 dozen rounds.

CHEDDAR CHEESE WAFERS

These crisp cheese wafers are easy to prepare and, if stored in a metal box in a cool place, will keep for months. Serve them hot or cold.

**1 cup grated strong cheddar
cheese
1 cup crushed potato chips
¼ cup soft butter
½ cup all-purpose flour
1 tsp. prepared mustard**

Measure the cheese and potato chips after grating or crushing. Place the cheese in a bowl with the remaining ingredients and blend. Place on an unbuttered baking sheet in small spoonfuls, flattening slightly with the bottom of the spoon.

Bake at 375° for 5-8 minutes or until golden brown. Cool on a cake rack. To serve hot, reheat at 300° for a few minutes.

PINK LADY DIP

Delicious when served with small cornmeal or oatmeal muffins (take out of freezer and warm up in 325°F. oven), cut into two or three pieces.

 1 cup mayonnaise
½ cup chili sauce
½ cup finely diced celery
 2 to 3 green onions, minced
   juice of 1 lemon
 2 hard-boiled eggs, minced

Mix together the mayonnaise, chili sauce, celery, green onions, and lemon juice. When well blended, add salt and pepper to taste. Place in a bowl and cover completely with the minced eggs. Refrigerate until ready to serve.

MUSHROOM ROLLS

These are served hot, 2 rolls per person. Prepare them ahead of time and keep refrigerated.

12 thin slices white bread
   soft butter
 ½ lb. finely chopped fresh
   mushrooms
 4 tbsp butter
 ½ tsp. curry powder
 1 tbsp. lemon juice
 ½ tsp. salt
 ¼ tsp. pepper

Remove crusts from bread and go over slices with a rolling pin to make them thinner. Spread with soft butter and set aside.

Melt 2 tablespoons of remaining butter with curry and lemon juice. Add mushrooms and sauté over high heat for 3 minutes, stirring constantly. Sprinkle with the salt and pepper.

Spread about 1 tablespoon of mushrooms over each slice of bread. Roll like a jelly roll, fasten each roll with picks, and place on a baking sheet. Melt last 2 tablespoons of butter, brush lightly over rolls, and refrigerate. When ready to serve, bake in a 425°F. oven for about 15 minutes, or until light brown. Serves 6.

LACE POTATO CRISPS

Make a week ahead. Cool. Wrap and freeze. To prepare, place frozen, one next to the other, on a baking sheet. Warm in a preheated 400°F. oven for 10 to 12 minutes or, until piping hot. Serve hot on a silver tray with small finger napkins.

> 1 large peeled potato, grated
> 1 medium-sized onion, grated
> ¼ tsp. salt
> ¼ tsp. savory
> salad oil

Grate and mix together the potato and the onion. Add the salt and savory.

Heat salad oil sizzling hot in an iron frying pan. Drop the mixture by small spoonfuls into the hot oil. It will cook quickly, about 30 seconds on each side. These potato crisps are very attractive; lacy, crisp and golden brown.

DAINTY BEEF ROLLS

These finger-sized rolls should be served hot with a half-and-half mixture of Dijon mustard and chili sauce and small fingers of crustless rye bread.

> ½ lb. ground round
> 1 medium onion, grated
> 2 eggs
> 2 tsp. curry powder
> ½ tsp. cumin seeds
> 4 tbsp. fine dry bread crumbs
> ½ cup chopped fresh parsley
> 1 tsp. salt
> salad oil

Place all ingredients, except the oil, in a bowl. Mix and knead until very smooth (or beat at medium speed in an electric mixer for 5 minutes). Work until the mixture is a smooth paste.

Wet your hands, take a small piece of the mixture and roll between your palms into the shape of a little finger. Set on wax paper until all the paste is rolled, then refrigerate.

To serve, heat oil in a frying pan over high heat. When hot, reduce the heat to medium (or place pan on another burner at medium heat if you have an electric stove). Add a few meat fingers at a time (don't crowd them), and fry until golden, about 3 - 4 minutes each. Serves 8 - 10.

13

CAVIAR TARTS

Slice bread very thinly and cut into 2-inch rounds with cookie cutter. Press into small, buttered muffin tins, brush with melted butter, and pinch edges of bread to form tart shapes. Bake in a 450°F. oven until crisp and brown, about 5 to 8 minutes. Cool, and store in a covered metal box. (They will keep 2 to 3 weeks.)

The Filling:
Cream 8 ounces of cream cheese with 1 tablespoon cream, and 1 green onion, finely minced. Put a small spoonful into each cup. Top with a blob of red or black caviar. Serve.

TERRINE DE CAMPAGNE

A terrine is a meat loaf with personality. A slice of this pâté served with crusty French bread and a glass of light red wine is an elegant hors d'oeuvre.

> 1 lb. lamb or pork liver
> 1 cup chopped onions
> 2 garlic cloves, crushed
> ¼ cup brandy
> ⅔ cup port wine
> ¼ lb. each, ground veal and pork
> 1½ tsp. salt
> ½ tsp. pepper
> 1 bay leaf
> 1 tsp. each, tarragon and thyme
> 2 eggs, beaten
> strips of side bacon

With a sharp knife, coarsely chop the liver (don't grind it) and place it in a non-metal bowl with the onion, garlic, brandy, and port. To marinate, cover and refrigerate for 24 hours.

Add all remaining ingredients, except bacon, and mix thoroughly (an electric mixer can be used at medium speed for 5 minutes).

Line a terrine or an 8 x 5-inch loaf pan with strips of bacon. Pour in meat mixture, place in a pan of hot water, and bake uncovered in a 350°F. oven for one hour. Turn heat down to 300°F. and bake 30 minutes.

Remove from oven, cover with foil or wax paper, and place a heavy object on top—the chefs use a brick, but a can of tomatoes or something like that will do. Refrigerate 12 hours, then unmold. A terrine will keep 2 - 3 weeks refrigerated, 2 months frozen. This recipe will serve 12.

Variations: Replace the veal and pork with an equal amount of raw wild or domestic duck. Or, when marinating the liver, add ½ lb. of coarsely chopped venison, sliced raw pheasant, or partridge breasts. Make terrine as indicated, layering thin slices of pheasant or partridge between liver mixture. The baking time remains the same.

CRABMEAT OR LOBSTER DIJON

Quick and good!

>1 cup commercial sour cream
>⅓ cup Dijon mustard
>2 tbsp. red wine vinegar or fresh
> lemon juice
>½ tsp. salt
>½ tsp. pepper
>2 cans well-drained lobster, crab,
> or fresh shellfish

Pour sour cream into a bowl. Combine the remaining ingredients and gradually blend into the cream, with a whisk or a hand beater.

Pour into an attractive bowl and surround it with the pieces of seafood.

BAKED GOLDEN SHRIMPS

This perfect hors d'oeuvre, or entrée, is especially good served in the garden before a barbecue. Uncooked shrimps are a must.

>1 lb. raw shrimps, unshelled
>1 tbsp. soy sauce
>2 tbsp. Worcestershire sauce,
> Chinese bean sauce, or brown
> sauce
>1 tbsp. sherry
>1 tbsp. brown sugar

Wash the shrimps in cold water and spread them on absorbent paper to dry. In a bowl, mix together the remaining ingredients, add the shrimps and marinate for 30 minutes.

Place shrimps and sauce in a pan and bake at 300° F. for 25 minutes. Serve in a hot earthenware dish, with plenty of napkins, and let each guest shell his own shrimps. Serves 4 - 6.

SHRIMPS IN BEER

These intriguing shrimps should really be surrounded by, and eaten with, raw vegetables: small sticks of carrots, celery, red and green peppers, cauliflower flowerets. But if that is too difficult, they are excellent without any embellishment.

>2 lbs. uncooked shrimps
>1 cup beer
>½ tsp. brown sugar
>2 green onions, chopped
>1 tsp. salt
>2 slices unpeeled lemon
>1 bay leaf
>2 parsley sprigs
> raw vegetables or fresh dill

15

Shell each shrimp before cooking by cutting along the soft underneath side, then pulling the shell apart. Place the remaining ingredients in a saucepan and simmer 10 minutes.

Add shrimps one by one, then stir with a fork until well mixed. Cover and simmer over very low heat about 5 minutes, or until shrimps are pink. Empty mixture into a bowl, cover, and let cool.

Refrigerate until ready to serve and drain before placing on platter. Surround with vegetables or sprinkle with dill.

LOBSTER DIP

Fresh shrimps can replace the fresh or canned lobster. (Even canned red sockeye salmon is good.)

    1 cup whipping cream
    ⅓ cup finely chopped lobster
      salt and pepper to taste
    ¼ tsp. curry powder
    2 tsp. brandy or sherry
    2 tbsp. chopped parsley or green
      onions

Whip the cream, season to taste with salt and pepper. Gently fold in the lobster. Stir the curry powder with the brandy. Blend in the cream with the chopped parsley or green onions. Yield: 1½ cups.

SEAFOOD HORS D'OEUVRES

Not economical, but a connoisseur selection. Serve with a glass of cold white wine. It will make the party.

    6 to 12 fresh oysters
    1 small jar red or black caviar
    1 tbsp. prepared horseradish
    2 limes or lemons
    2 lbs. uncooked shrimps
    1 to 2 lbs. fresh or frozen lobster
    1 avocado
    4 green onions, minced
    4 tbsp. fresh minced parsley
    ½ tsp. fresh ground pepper
    6 tbsp. salad oil
    2 tbsp. wine or cider vinegar
    ½ tsp. H.P. sauce
    ⅛ to ¼ tsp. Tabasco
    ½ tsp. salt
    ¼ tsp. curry powder or tarragon
    1 tbsp. brandy or rye

Fill a large attractive platter with crushed ice and set it in the freezer, or prepare the platter when ready to serve.

In the middle, place the oysters on the half shell. Blend together the caviar and the prepared horseradish, and place this mixture carefully and evenly on each oyster. Quarter the limes or the lemons and set on ice around the oysters. If you have the patience to do it, wrap each quarter of lime or lemon with a small square of cheesecloth to prevent splattering when the fruit is squeezed.

Bring 4 cups of water to a fast boil. Add 2 slices of unpeeled lemon and ½ teaspoon salt. Add the uncooked shrimps, lower heat, and simmer exactly 5 minutes. Remove from heat, cool the shrimps in their water, remove shells. Place in a bowl, cover and refrigerate until ready to use.

To serve, place here and there and in between the lemon or lime quarters. Put a colored pick in each shrimp. Thaw out the lobster overnight in the refrigerator. Wrap lobster pieces tightly in absorbent paper, so the excess water is absorbed.

Cut the avocado pears in half, remove stones and place one half on each side of the platter.

Mix together the onions, parsley, pepper, salad oil, vinegar, H.P. sauce, Tabasco, salt, curry powder or tarragon and brandy or rye. Pour some into the cavity of each avocado. Reserve balance to refill avocado. This is the dipping sauce for the shrimps and lobster. Place lobster on each side of platter. Tuna fish, crabmeat, clams, squares of poached halibut, etc. can be added.

This may seem involved, but in reality it is simple, as everything can be ready and waiting in the refrigerator. All there is to do is to set it attractively on a large deep platter filled with crushed ice.

This hors d'oeuvre served with white wine is delicious. You will need small plates and small picks or forks. Another requisite is a large bundle of paper napkins.

OLAF HORS D'OEUVRES

For an attractive hors d'oeuvre before a small dinner, make a circle of parsley with a heart of lemon wedges on a plate and surround with eggs done as follows:

> 1 can sardines
> 6 hard-boiled eggs
> 2 tbsp. relish or chutney
> peel of ½ lemon, grated
> 2 tbsp. mayonnaise
> pimiento strips

Cut hard-boiled eggs in half lengthwise. Scoop out yolks and mash with relish or chutney, lemon peel and mayonnaise. Salt and pepper to taste and stuff whites with the mixture. Top each half with a sardine and decorate with 2 thin strips of pimiento crisscrossed over the top. Refrigerate until ready to serve, then place each egg half on a crisp lettuce leaf. Serves 6.

SARDINE AND CHEESE FINGERS

These are tasty and simple appetizers to serve with beer or, as a side dish with a salad. Prepare and refrigerate until ready to bake.

> **4 slices white bread, toasted**
> **6 tbsp. cheese, grated**
> **12 small sardines**
> **parsley, chopped**
> **capers or small pickles**
> **lemon juice**

Remove crust from toasted bread and cut each slice into 3 fingers. Generously butter a shallow baking dish and arrange fingers in it. Sprinkle each one with grated cheese, then place a sardine on top. Sprinkle with a bit of parsley, place a few capers on each sardine, then a few drops of lemon juice. Dot with small dice of butter and top with grated cheese. Bake in middle of a 425°F. oven for 8 - 10 minutes or until cheese melts. Serves 4.

PICKLED WILD MUSHROOMS

This recipe was a contribution of the English settlers to Upper Canada's traditional cuisine. Gathering wild mushrooms is a lost art, but this old recipe can be used for cultivated mushrooms with equal success. It makes a most pleasant hors d'oeuvre or pickle.

Tie up in a piece of cheesecloth: several strips of parsley, pinch of thyme, a bay leaf, a whole clove, a dozen peppercorns. Put these in a saucepan with 2 cups water, 1 cup olive oil, ½ cup vinegar (I sometimes like to use lemon juice instead of vinegar). Boil 5 minutes. Then add 1 lb. button mushrooms, the stems neatly clipped off, and let it all boil for 15 minutes. Remove from heat, take away spice bag, let mushrooms cool in juice. Pot, seal, and keep in a cool, dark place.

CHAPTER 2

SOUPS

Selecting the right soup is important, but just as important is the way it is presented or garnished.

I usually like to serve my soup directly at the table – from a tureen, which can be anything from a costly soup tureen to a flowerpot holder. The plates, biscuits, garnish, and serving spoon are all placed in front of me, which saves many steps back and forth to the kitchen.

As we live in a fast-moving age, we often turn to canned soups; well combined and well presented, they can be very nice. Whether you serve a consommé, bouillon, cream, or bisque, either homemade or canned, try some of the following ideas for a more elegant soup presentation.

Slightly salted whipped cream
Minced fresh mint and almonds
Grated cucumber stirred with lime juice
Sizzling hot-buttered croutons rolled in Parmesan cheese
Grated egg yolks and parsley, mixed
Grated egg whites and chives, mixed
Finely grated raw carrots and lemon rind

Any of the above suggestions can be used on clear or cream, hot or cold soups. They are elegant, tasty and different.

How to Make Stock
BEEF STOCK OR BOUILLON

A good stock is the basis for hundreds of delectable soups, sauces, and other dishes. Although the preparation is a bit time consuming, it is not complicated, and you can let it simmer slowly without having to watch it.

2 tbsp. beef fat or butter
2 lbs. brisket or shoulder of beef
1 to 2 lbs. veal knuckle
3 quarts tepid water
4 medium onions, quartered
2 whole carrots
3 whole cloves
1 tbsp. coarse salt
½ tsp. dry mustard
½ tsp. thyme
1 cup celery leaves, chopped

Melt the beef fat or butter in a soup kettle, and brown the beef in it. Add the remaining ingredients. Bring to a boil. Skim. Cover and simmer over low heat for 2½ hours.

To strain the consommé, spread a damp cloth over a large bowl. Empty the contents of the soup kettle into the cloth. Let it drain without touching. This takes only a few seconds. Pour into milk bottles, cover and refrigerate. When the consommé cools, the fat will rise to the top and harden, which prevents air from penetrating and the consommé may be kept, refrigerated, from 2 to 3 weeks. If frozen, it will keep for 6 to 7 months. Yield: 3 quarts.

CHICKEN CONSOMMÉ

Use the leftover cooked chicken meat for salad or chicken pie. As it is difficult to find a truly good chicken consommé, I recommend keeping some on hand. It will keep refrigerated or frozen for the same amount of time as basic beef consommé.

4 lb. boiling fowl
butter
6 cups cold water
1 carrot, sliced
2 stalks celery
1 clove garlic, chopped
½ bay leaf
¼ tsp. peppercorns
¼ tsp. thyme
1 tbsp. coarse salt
1 onion, finely minced

Cut up the chicken and brown the pieces lightly in a little butter. Transfer to a soup kettle and add the remaining ingredients. Cover and bring to a boil. Simmer for 1½ to 2 hours or until the chicken is tender.

Strain the same way as for basic beef consommé. Keep refrigerated. Yield: 6 cups.

Hot Soups

CONSOMMÉ PRINTANIÈRE

Boiling hot chicken consommé is poured over paper-thin slices of fresh vegetables to cook them. It is then served without delay. A delicate, superlative spring soup.

4 radishes
½ medium cucumber, peeled
½ small zucchini, unpeeled
1 small carrot, peeled
2 small inner stalks celery
6 cups chicken bouillon
1 tbsp. finely chopped fresh
    tarragon or chives

Cut vegetables as thinly as possible. Place in warmed-up soup tureen. Bring the chicken bouillon to a rapid boil. Pour over the vegetables. Sprinkle the tarragon or chives on top. Serve at once. Serves 6.

POTAGE À LA REINE

This recipe was created by Taillerent (1314 to 1395), the first of the French chefs. He wrote the first *Viandier*, which is the oldest known cookbook.

4 to 6 lb. boiling chicken
¼ tsp. celery seeds
¼ tsp. peppercorns
¼ tsp. thyme
1 tsp. dry mustard
2 onions, minced
1 clove garlic, minced
1 tbsp. salt
2 quarts water
1½ cups light cream or milk
3 egg yolks, beaten
2 tbsp. soft butter
½ cup toasted shredded almonds

Place in a saucepan the chicken, celery seeds, peppercorns, thyme, dry mustard, onions, garlic, salt and water. Bring to a boil, cover, and simmer over low heat for 1½ to 2 hours or until the chicken is tender. Cook until tepid. When ready, remove chicken, take the meat from the bones, and remove the skin. Chop the chicken meat very fine, or, place in a blender with the cream, egg yolks, and soft butter. Cover and blend until creamy, ½ to one minute.

When chopped by hand, add the ingredients to the chopped chicken.

Strain the consommé, add the chicken mixture and stir over low heat until hot, but do not boil. Serve in cups with a spoonful of toasted almonds in each cup. Serves 6.

CREAM BORDELAISE

A French classic with a beautiful color and a superb taste. Nothing quick about it, but well worth the effort involved.

2 lbs. fresh green peas
1 head of Boston lettuce
2 cups well flavored chicken broth
salt and pepper
½ chicken breast, cut into
matchsticks
3 egg yolks
1 cup hot light cream

Wash the peas in the pods. With scissors, cut off the tips of the pods at both ends. Place the trimmed pods in a saucepan, pour boiling water on top, and boil fast for 15 to 20 minutes. Drain through a sieve.

In the meantime, wash the lettuce and chop it into fine shreds. Place in a pan and pour boiling water on top. Let stand for 10 minutes, away from heat.

Remove the peas from the pods and pour the peas into the hot chicken broth. Drain the lettuce and add to the peas. Add salt and pepper to taste. Simmer together for 15 minutes.

Simmer the shreds of chicken breast in a little extra chicken broth for 20 minutes. Add to the green peas.

Place the egg yolks in a soup tureen and beat lightly with a whisk. Pour the boiling hot cream on top of the eggs while beating with a whisk. Add the pea soup. Stir. Taste for seasoning and serve. Serves 6.

CHICKEN BITS AND PIECES SOUP

A versatile, economical soup. Use the first part only as a chicken bouillon, or serve it as a cream soup. For everyday use, garnish with parsley or thin slivers of celery; for guests, top with a sprig of watercress or small cubes of avocado or toasted slivered almonds.

2 lbs. mixed chicken backs and
wings
6 cups water
1 stalk celery with leaves
1 bay leaf
½ tsp. tarragon or thyme
1 onion, sliced
1 tsp. salt
6 peppercorns
1 cup light cream
1 cup milk
3 tbsp. butter
3 tbsp. flour

Place in a saucepan the chicken pieces, water, celery, bay leaf, tarragon or thyme, onion, salt, and peppercorns. Bring to a boil, cover, then simmer for 2 hours. Strain. Remove and discard the skin and bones. Reserve the meat.

Place the broth in a clean saucepan, add the cream and milk, bring to boil. Make a ball with the butter and flour, add to boiling soup, and stir until creamy. Add the chicken meat. Taste for seasoning. Garnish and serve. Serves 6.

DREPSLEY CHICKEN SOUP

Drepsleys are very tiny dumplings referred to as "rivels" in western Canada and "drepsleys" in Ontario.

1 3-lb. chicken
½ cup chopped celery leaves
1 bay leaf
10 peppercorns
1¼ tsp. salt
5 cups hot water
1 cup diced celery
2 tbsp. chopped fresh parsley
2 tbsp. butter
2 eggs
5-6 tbsp. flour

Cut the chicken into portions. Place the pieces in a saucepan with celery leaves, bay leaf, peppercorns, one teaspoon of the salt and the hot water.

Bring to a boil, cover, and simmer over low heat for about one hour or until chicken is tender. Strain, then return broth to saucepan.

Cut chicken into small pieces and add to broth with diced celery and parsley. Bring again to a simmer.

To make the drepsleys, cream the butter, add the eggs, and beat. Gradually add the flour and the remaining ¼ teaspoon of salt. Beat hard until the mixture is like very soft butter. Drop by ¼ or ½ teaspoon into simmering soup. Cover the pan and let stand over low heat for 5 minutes or until the tiny dumplings are cooked. Serves 6.

SHERRIED CREAM OF MUSHROOM SOUP

If you have a blender, by all means use it for this gourmet soup.

½ lb. fresh mushrooms, sliced
1 stick celery, diced
1 small onion, sliced
1 cup chicken bouillon
3 tbsp. butter
2 tbsp. flour
1¼ cups milk
1 cup light cream
2 tbsp. dry sherry
salt to taste
juice of ½ lemon

Place in a blender the mushrooms, celery, onion, and chicken bouillon

23

(1 cup hot water and 1 bouillon cube can replace homemade bouillon). Cover and blend at medium speed for 2 minutes.

CREAM OF CABBAGE SOUP

Serve this hearty and delicious soup as the French do – in large, deep soup plates.

1 onion, chopped
2 carrots, diced
2 celery stalks, tops only, chopped
1 large potato, peeled and diced
2 cups boiling water
4 cups milk, scalded
2-3 cups cabbage, finely shredded
1 tsp. salt
½ tsp. pepper
2 tbsp. butter

In a saucepan, combine the onion, carrots, celery and potato. Pour the boiling water on top, then cover and simmer over medium-low heat for 20 minutes, or until the potato is tender.

Mash the vegetables with a fork, but do not worry if some stay whole.

Add the scalded milk and bring to a fast rolling boil. Add the cabbage, salt and pepper. Simmer, uncovered, for 10-15 minutes. Add the butter and season to taste. To serve this *à l'Italienne*, fry 6 slices of bread in butter, then place one in the bottom of each soup plate. Sprinkle with grated Parmesan cheese and pour the soup on top. Serves 6.

HOT TOMATO BOUILLON

This is my favorite beginning to a cold meal.

16-oz. can tomato juice
1 tsp. butter
2 tsp. lemon juice
¼ tsp. grated lemon peel
salt and pepper, to taste
¼ cup whipping cream
¼ tsp. curry powder

Heat the tomato juice, then add the butter, lemon juice and lemon peel. When the mixture is boiling, add salt and pepper.

Just before serving, whip the cream with the curry powder and use this golden cream to top each cup of hot bouillon. If you serve it without the cream, simply add the curry powder to the bouillon. Serves 4.

TOMATO SOUP "DE MA TANTE"

I have never tasted a better fresh tomato soup than this one, which was the delight of my younger days and still is. My aunt always used fresh basil.

24 medium-sized sweet red tomatoes
1 tbsp. sugar
2 tbsp. butter
1 onion, quartered
2 bay leaves
2 celery ribs with leaves
1 tbsp. minced fresh basil or
   crumbled dried basil
1 tsp. salt
¼ tsp. freshly ground pepper
3 tbsp. minced fresh parsley
   juice of ½ lemon
½ cup whipped cream

Cut the unpeeled tomatoes into quarters. Place in a heavy metal saucepan with the sugar, butter, onion, bay leaves, celery, and basil. Cover and simmer over low heat for 30 minutes. Do not add water at any time. Pass through a food mill or a sieve. Put back in the saucepan and add the salt, pepper, parsley and lemon juice. Simmer for a few minutes. Taste for seasoning. Serve in cups, topped with a spoonful of whipped cream, slightly salted. Serves 8 or more.

TOURIN PROVENÇAL

French olive oil should be used for this soup and fresh tomatoes are a must. Serve in white or pink porcelain cups.

4 tbsp. olive oil or butter
4 large onions, cut in slices
4 large tomatoes, thickly sliced
1 tsp. sugar
6 cups hot water
1 clove garlic, crushed
1 bay leaf
¼ tsp. thyme
   salt and pepper, to taste
½ cup fine vermicelli
¼ cup fresh chopped parsley

Heat the olive oil or melt the butter in a saucepan. Add the onions and tomatoes. Simmer 5 to 10 minutes or until onions are limp. Add hot water, garlic, bay leaf, thyme, salt, and pepper. Bring to a boil, cover, then simmer over low heat for one hour. At this point, the *tourin* can be strained to make a bouillon or left as is, which is the classic way. Add the vermicelli, simmer until soft, taste for seasoning, add parsley, and serve. Serves 6.

GREEN TOMATO SOUP

An old-fashioned special – not to be forgotten.

    3 cups green tomatoes, unpeeled
      and chopped
    1 onion, chopped
    ¼ tsp. cinnamon
    ⅛ tsp. ground cloves
    1 tsp. sugar
    ¼ tsp. pepper
    4 cups water
    ¼ tsp. soda
    3 tbsp. butter
    3 tbsp. all-purpose flour
    4 cups milk

Place in a saucepan the tomatoes, onion, cinnamon, ground cloves, sugar, pepper, and water. Bring to a boil and boil for 20 minutes. Add the soda.

Melt the butter and add flour. Mix and add the milk. Cook until creamy, stirring constantly. Add the green tomatoes to the cream. Mix thoroughly. Salt to taste and serve. Serves 6-8.

CUCUMBER BISQUE

A cream of cucumber soup, served hot and garnished with diced raw cucumber. It has a fresh spring flavor.

    2 medium onions, chopped
    2 cucumbers, peeled and chopped
    4 tbsp. butter
    2 cups water or chicken bouillon
    2 tbsp. flour
    2 egg yolks
    ½ cup heavy cream
    1 small cucumber, peeled and diced
      salt and pepper, to taste

Melt the butter in saucepan, add the cucumber and onion and simmer uncovered over low heat until the onions are transparent. Add the water or bouillon and boil gently until the vegetables are tender, about 20 minutes.

Then pass through a sieve or, better still, pour into a blender and blend for 40 seconds.

When made in the blender, add the flour, egg yolks, and cream. Cover, blend one minute. Simmer over low heat until thickened and creamy.

When done in the sieve, melt 2 tablespoons of butter in a saucepan, add the flour. Stir until mixed, add the puréed vegetables, and stir constantly over medium heat until creamy. Beat the egg yolks and cream together and stir into the hot soup. Simmer 5 minutes over low heat, stirring often.

To serve, garnish each plate with a spoonful of the diced raw cucumber. Serves 4 to 5.

FRENCH PUMPKIN SOUP

One of the most delicious ways to have pumpkin.

3 tbsp. butter
2 lbs. pumpkin, peeled and diced
¼ tsp. grated mace
1 cup water
1 cup milk
½ cup light cream
1½ tsp. salt
¼ tsp. pepper
½ cup fried bread croutons

Melt the butter and add the pumpkin and mace. Stir, cover, and simmer over low heat for 20 minutes. Add water and milk and bring to a boil. Cover and simmer for 10 minutes longer. Force through a sieve and add the cream, salt, and pepper. Heat just to boiling, but do not let it boil. Serve with the croutons. Serves 6.

POTAGE "ESAU"

Lentil soup is not everyday fare, but whenever I serve it, guests always rave about it. This is a cream or potage of lentils.

1 cup whole green lentils
6 cups cold water
1 onion, cut in four
1 clove garlic, crushed
½ tsp. freshly ground pepper
1 cup heavy cream
1 to 3 tbsp. wine or cider vinegar

Wash the lentils in a colander under running cold water. Place in a bowl or saucepan. Add the water and soak for 2 hours.

Add the onion, garlic, and pepper. (Do not salt at this point, as it would harden the lentils.) Slowly bring to boil and simmer, covered, for about one hour or until lentils are soft.

Then rub through a sieve or blend in an electric blender, in both cases using only half the liquid.

Thin the puréed lentils with the rest of the cooking liquid to the consistency of a fairly thick soup. Salt to taste and reheat to boiling point. Gradually stir in the cream. Heat, but do not boil. Add vinegar to taste and serve very hot with a sprinkling of fresh parsley. Serves 6.

MY LENTIL SOUP

Meatless and so good.

2 cups brown lentils
4 cups cold water
2 tbsp. salt
¼ tsp. pepper
½ cup butter
1 large can (1 lb. 13 oz.) tomatoes
1 large onion, diced
2 tbsp. fresh dill or 1 tbsp. dill
seeds
2 garlic cloves, crushed
2 bay leaves

Place all the ingredients in a saucepan. Slowly bring to a boil. Cover and simmer over low heat for 2 to 2½ hours. Serves 6.

SUMMER VEGETABLE SOUP

My Finnish friend, Marta, showed me how to make this marvelous soup, which should only be made with succulent young vegetables, if possible, fresh from the garden.

10 to 15 tiny new carrots
1 cup fresh green peas
2 cups green or wax beans, cut into
2-inch pieces
2 to 4 green onions, chopped
2 cups tiny new potatoes, grated
1 tbsp. sugar
1 tsp. salt
2 tbsp. flour
4 cups milk
2 tbsp. butter
¼ cup chopped parsley

If tiny carrots and potatoes are unavailable, replace them with 3 medium-sized carrots, cut into 2-inch sticks, and 2 cups cubed medium potatoes.

Place the carrots, peas, beans, onions, and potatoes in a pot. Add boiling water, just to cover the vegetables. Boil, uncovered, for 5 minutes.

In another saucepan, place the sugar, salt, flour, and milk. Whisk until well blended, then bring to a boil, stirring. Pour the liquid over the vegetables and simmer for 10 minutes. Add the butter and parsley. Serve hot. Serves 5 to 6.

VEGETABLE CHEESE SOUP

Excellent for a company dinner. Serve with small bowls of grated cheese and finely chopped chives or parsley.

⅔ cup carrots, grated
½ cup celery, finely diced
⅓ cup chopped green onions
¼ cup butter
⅓ cup flour
2 cups chicken bouillon or
2 cups water with 2 chicken cubes
2 cups light cream or milk
¼ tsp. salt
1 cup grated old cheddar cheese
1 tbsp. brandy

Place in saucepan the carrots, celery, onions, and butter. Stir until well coated with the butter, then cook over low heat until soft but not browned. Blend in the flour. Stir in the bouillon, or water and cubes, then the milk or cream. Cook and stir, over medium heat, until mixture comes to boil and thickens. Add the salt, cheese, and brandy. Heat just enough to melt the cheese. Serve. Yield: about 1 quart.

COUNTRY BEAN SOUP

If you can't get a ham bone, ask your butcher for ham or bacon rind, or use 1 or 2 thin ham steaks, diced, or 3 or 4 sliced frankfurters.

1 lb. dried navy beans
3 quarts cold water
1 ham bone or substitute
1 cup celery, chopped
1 large onion, diced
3 carrots, thinly sliced
1 tbsp. salt
½ tsp. pepper
1 cup tomato juice

Wash the beans and place them in a large saucepan. Cover with the cold water and let stand overnight to soak.

The next morning, bring the beans and water to a fast rolling boil over high heat. Add the ham bone, or substitute, cover, and simmer over low heat for 2 hours. Add the remaining ingredients and simmer, covered, for one more hour or until the beans are tender. Makes about 3 quarts.

CREAM OF SPLIT PEA

A delightful soup and a very nourishing way to use a ham bone. When possible, flavor the soup with fresh mint, although dried mint may also be used.

1½ cups split green peas
6 cups hot water
1 ham bone
1 onion, finely chopped
½ cup celery, diced
2 cups milk
1 tbsp. butter
1 tsp. fresh mint, minced
salt and pepper, to taste

Rinse the split peas and soak them overnight in enough cold water to cover. The next day, drain and place the peas in a large saucepan and add the hot water, ham bone, onion, and celery. Cover and simmer over low heat for 2 hours, stirring occasionally.

Remove the ham bone and pass through a sieve or a food mill. Put the purée back into the saucepan and add the milk, butter, mint, salt, and pepper.

Simmer for a few minutes and serve with buttered croutons. Serves 6.

FROZEN GREEN PEA SOUP

You'll find that this soup, even without meat, is sufficiently nourishing to serve as a light main course. It is a simplified version of Crème St. Germain.

1 chicken bouillon cube
1 cup water
1 pkg. frozen green peas
1 small onion, diced
1 tbsp. butter
2 tbsp. flour
3 cups milk, or 1½ cups milk and
   1½ cups cream
salt and pepper, to taste

Add the bouillon cube to the water and bring to a boil. Then add the frozen green peas and boil for 10 minutes, or until the peas are tender.

Make a purée of the peas, either in an electric blender or by pressing them through a sieve. While the peas are cooking, lightly fry the onion in the butter. Add the flour, blend, then add the milk. Stir until smooth and add the puréed peas. Mix well, add salt and pepper, and serve piping hot.

If you wish, sprinkle the soup with chopped fresh mint or crumbled dried mint. Serves 6.

CLASSIC ONION SOUP

Unsalted butter, beef stock, and dry French bread are the secrets of this good soup.

> **2 lbs. (about 8 medium) onions**
> **4 - 6 tbsp. butter, unsalted**
> **6 cups beef stock or consommé**
> **6 thick slices of dry, crusty French**
> **bread**
> **1 cup Swiss cheese, cut into slivers**

Peel and slice the onions as thinly as possible. Melt the butter in a heavy metal saucepan and, when light brown, add the onions. Cook 20 minutes over low heat, stirring 5 to 6 times. Keep uncovered the first 10 minutes and covered the last 10 minutes. The onions must be limp or softened, but not browned; this is very important in the preparation of classic French onion soup.

When the onions are limp and full of a delicate aroma, add the beef stock or consommé. When using canned consommé, dilute according to directions on can.

Bring to a boil and season to taste. Simmer, uncovered, 20 to 30 minutes. Classic onion soup is never boiled or cooked over high heat, but is simmered slowly to perfect goodness. When the soup is ready, place in individual earthenware casseroles (or a large one) and top with bread prepared in the following manner: Toast each slice of bread, butter lightly, and cover thickly with the slivers of Swiss cheese. Gently place on top of the soup and put in a 500°F. oven until cheese is puffy and golden brown. Serves 6.

The soup can be prepared ahead of time and reheated. The bread can also be prepared ahead of time and placed on the hot soup when ready to serve.

Les Halles' onion soup differs from the classic soup only by the addition of 2 cups of milk, added at the same time as the consommé. If you wish, 2 tablespoons of flour can be sprinkled over the onions before adding consommé.

ONION SOUP ILE-DE-FRANCE

Should wine be used in onion soup? This has remained an unanswered question among gourmets for many years. I like it for a winter buffet or an elegant dinner.

> **8 large onions, thinly sliced**
> **⅓ cup butter**
> **½ cup all-purpose flour**
> **4 cups water**
> **1 bottle dry white wine**
> **¼ tsp. thyme**
> **salt and pepper, to taste**
> **12 thin slices French bread**
> **Parmesan cheese, grated**

Melt 4 tbsp. of the butter in a heavy metal saucepan. Add the onions, stir until they are coated with butter. Cover pan and simmer 15 minutes over low heat. Remove from pan and set aside.

Add the remaining butter to the pan, stir in the flour and cook over medium heat, stirring most of the time, until the flour turns golden brown. Add the water and the wine all at once. Beat well and stir constantly over high heat until boiling and slightly thickened. Add the onions, thyme, salt, and pepper. Cover and simmer for 25 minutes. Serves 12.

AUVERGNE ONION SOUP

In Auvergne, it is called *la bolée*. Quick and economical to make, it is one of my most treasured recipes, dating back to my student days in Paris.

6 onions, thinly sliced
1 quart water
1 tsp. salt
¼ tsp. pepper
  pinch of thyme
4 tbsp. farina (cream of wheat)
3 tbsp. melted chicken fat or butter
2 egg yolks
3 tbsp. rich or sour cream
¼ tsp. celery salt
¼ cup fresh parsley, finely chopped

Bring the water to a full rolling boil with salt, pepper, and thyme. Add the farina while beating with a whisk or rotary beater. Simmer over very low heat for 8 minutes.

Melt the chicken fat or butter, add the onions and simmer, uncovered, over low heat until the onions are soft. Add to the water and simmer for 10 minutes. (This first part can be cooked ahead of time.)

To serve, place the egg yolks in a soup tureen or earthenware casserole, add the cream, and beat together until well blended. Pour the boiling hot soup on top, beating all the while. Add the celery salt and parsley. Serves 4-5.

In Auvergne, the 2 egg whites are cooked in a frying pan in a bit of butter. When cooked, they are cooled and sliced, or chopped, and used as a garnish on top of the soup.

BEEF AND BARLEY SOUP

This soup sticks to the ribs on cold winter days.

1 cup hulled barley
3 quarts cold water
2 lbs. brisket of beef or 1
   roast-beef bone
1 tbsp. coarse salt
2 carrots, sliced
1 large onion, thinly sliced
2 stalks celery, diced
2 leeks, thinly sliced (optional)
½ tsp. thyme
½ tsp. savory
1 lemon

Place barley in a bowl and cover with tepid water. Let soak for one hour. (Do not use pearl barley for this soup.)

Place the cold water, beef brisket or bone, and the coarse salt in a soup kettle. Add the drained barley. Bring to a boil over low heat, and remove the first scum with a skimmer. When the water reaches a rapid boil, add ½ cup cold water, which will slow down the boiling and allow the balance of the scum to reach the top, so that it can be removed. This is important, as here lies the difference between a barley soup with a good color and one with a greyish dirty color. Serves 8-10.

CREAM OF CLAM SOUP

Either homemade or canned chicken broth can be used to make this tasty soup.

1 can (10½ oz.) minced clams
1 cup light cream
2 cups chicken broth
2 tbsp. lemon juice
½ cup white wine or sherry
   sprinkling of paprika

Drain the clams. Place in container of electric blender with the cream. Blend until mixture is smooth.

Heat with the chicken broth, lemon juice, and wine or sherry. Serve hot with a sprinkling of paprika. Serves 4.

POTAGE ST. GERMAIN

Often made with split green peas, the true St. Germain is made with fresh green peas or, as a second choice, frozen green peas. Equally good hot or cold.

> 3 cups shelled fresh peas (about 3 lbs.), or,
> 3 cups frozen green peas
> 2 heads of Boston or large bibb lettuce
> 2 small leeks, cleaned and sliced
> 4 cups water
> salt, to taste
> 2 tbsp. butter
> ½ cup rich or light cream

Place in a saucepan the shelled fresh peas or frozen peas, the coarsely shredded lettuce and the leeks. Add the water and salt. Bring to a boil, then cook over medium heat until peas are tender: 15 minutes for fresh peas, 10 minutes for frozen peas. Drain the vegetables and reserve the liquid.

Pass the vegetables through a strainer or a *presse-purée*. Return the purée to the saucepan and thin to the desired consistency with the reserved liquid. Bring to a boil again then gradually add the butter and the cream, beating constantly. Taste for seasoning and serve at once. To serve cold, omit the butter and add the cream when ready to serve. Serves 4 to 6.

Chowders

The word "chowder" comes from the French *la chaudière*, which means cauldron or big copper pot which was used on hinges to cook in the fireplace. It now means a sturdy, nourishing type of soup, usually made from fish or shellfish, canned or fresh. The most famous is clam chowder, for which the three essential ingredients are potatoes, fish, and salt pork. It is a meal in itself, usually served with large toasted and buttered pilot crackers.

MY MOTHER'S CLAM CHOWDER

I learned to make and enjoy chowder from this recipe.

½ cup diced salt pork
1 cup peeled, diced raw potatoes
2 large onions, minced
1 can (20 oz.) tomatoes
1 can (10 oz.) minced or large clams
1 tbsp. sugar
1 tbsp. salt
½ tsp. curry powder

Cook the salt pork over low heat in a saucepan, until crisp and brown. Add the onions and potatoes and stir together 5 to 8 minutes. Add the tomatoes, the liquid drained from the clams, sugar, salt, and curry. Bring to a boil. Cover and simmer over low heat for 30 minutes. Add the clams. Serve boiling hot with a jug of cold rich cream – each person adds it to his own plate of chowder. Serves 6.

CORN CHOWDER

A good choice for a quick lunch when it is cold outside, as this is a thick and satisfying chowder.

        8 slices bacon
        4 medium onions, sliced
        6 potatoes, cubed in ½-inch pieces
        5 cups milk
        ½ tsp. marjoram
          salt and pepper, to taste
        2 cups corn niblets
        1 tbsp. butter

Fry the bacon in a frying pan until crisp. Remove from pan and pour the fat into a saucepan. Add the onions to the fat and cook until golden brown. Add the potatoes, milk, marjoram, salt, and pepper. Cook, covered, over medium-low heat until the potatoes are tender, about 30 to 40 minutes. Add corn and butter. Simmer for 10 minutes. Stir in the crunchy bacon bits when ready to serve and taste for seasoning. Serves 6.

CELERY CHOWDER

This creamy nourishing soup does justice to the light flavor of celery.

        1½ cups diced celery
        ¼ cup chopped celery leaves
        1 large potato, peeled and diced
        2 cups boiling water
        1 tsp. salt
        ½ tsp. pepper
        ¼ tsp. marjoram
        2 cups milk
        2 tbsp. butter
        1 hard-boiled egg, chopped

Simmer the vegetables, water, and seasonings uncovered over medium heat until celery and potatoes are very tender – about 30 minutes.

Mash mixture in the saucepan with a fork, then add the milk and butter and simmer uncovered for 10 minutes. Add egg at the last moment. Serves 4 - 5.

NOVA SCOTIA CRABMEAT CHOWDER

Nova Scotia packages very good frozen crabmeat which makes excellent chowder. Lacking this, replace with an equal quantity of canned crabmeat.

3 slices salt pork
1 large onion, sliced thin
2 cups sliced potatoes
1½ cups hot water
3 cups hot milk
1 lb. frozen or canned (16 oz.)
  crabmeat
¼ tsp. savory
2 tbsp. butter

Cut the salt pork into 1½-inch squares. Melt and brown over medium heat in a large saucepan.

Make alternate layers of potatoes and onions over the browned pork and fat. Add the hot water. Cover. Bring to a boil and simmer from 10 to 15 minutes or until the potatoes are tender. Add the milk, crabmeat, savory, and butter. Do not stir, simply keep warm until ready to serve. Taste for seasoning. Serves 4.

OYSTER CHOWDER

Another super delight, the very best oyster chowder I have ever eaten.

½ cup butter
1 cup celery, chopped
1 cup carrots, finely grated
1 medium-sized onion, minced
1 leek, thinly sliced
¼ cup butter
½ cup flour
1 pint milk
1 pint light cream
1 pint oysters, fresh or canned
1 can clam juice or minced clams
½ cup white wine or dry sherry
  salt and pepper, to taste

Melt the ½ cup butter, add celery, carrots, onion, and leek and stir until well coated with the butter. Cover and simmer for 20 minutes over very low heat, stirring once or twice.

Make a white sauce with the ¼ cup butter, flour, milk, and cream, stirring all the time until thick and creamy. Add the vegetables, salt, and pepper. Mix well and set aside until ready to serve.

To serve, bring the clam juice or minced clams to a boil, add the oysters and their water, and the sherry or white wine. Cook over low heat for about 10 minutes, being careful not to let the mixture boil. When very hot, pour into the cream sauce, stir over low heat until hot, and serve. Serves 10 to 12.

FRENCH FISH CHOWDER

This is a type of bouillabaisse, although simpler and easier to make, and completely different in flavor from the previous chowders.

2 to 3 lbs. mixed salt-water fish
  (flounder, haddock, cod, shrimp)
2 fresh tomatoes, thinly sliced
2 leeks, cleaned and chopped
2 large onions, thinly sliced
1 stalk celery, diced
½ cup olive or salad oil
1 cup white wine
1-3 cloves garlic, crushed
2 bay leaves
½ tsp. thyme
1 tsp. salt
½ tsp. pepper
8 cups boiling water
1 small envelope saffron (optional)
½ cup vermicelli

Place in a saucepan the tomatoes, leeks, onions, celery, oil, and white wine. Season with the garlic, bay leaves, thyme, salt, and pepper. Cook over high heat, uncovered, about 10 to 15 minutes, stirring occasionally.

Gradually add the boiling water, then the fish. Cover and simmer over low heat for one hour.

Remove from heat and pass through a sieve, pressing out ingredients as much as possible. Put liquid back in the cleaned saucepan. Add the vermicelli and the saffron. Cover and simmer for 15 minutes. Serves 6 to 8.

FRESH SALMON CHOWDER

Every spring when we have fresh Gaspé salmon, we use the neck portion and the trimmings to make the finest of all chowders. This is another family recipe.

2 lbs. fresh salmon
1 cup water
1 large onion, chopped fine
2 tbsp. butter
2 cups potatoes, peeled and cut into
  ½ inch cubes
1 tsp. salt
¼ tsp. basil
  a pinch each, thyme and
  marjoram
3 tbsp. fresh parsley, chopped
1 cup light cream
1 cup hot milk
5 soda crackers, crushed
2 tbsp. butter

Place the salmon and water into a saucepan. Bring to a boil, then simmer until tender (about 8 to 12 minutes). Be careful not to overcook. Drain and reserve liquid. Remove skin, bones, and dark part from fish. Break remaining fish into pieces.

Fry the onion in the butter over medium heat. Boil the potatoes in enough hot water to cover, for 5 minutes. Drain and add the onions and potatoes to the fish. Add the salt, basil, thyme, marjoram, and parsley and simmer for 5 minutes. Cover and simmer 10 minutes more, then add the cream, milk, crackers, and butter. Heat, but do not boil. Serve piping hot. Serves 6.

Cold Soups

PERFECT MADRILÈNE

This is gourmet fare when clarified and jellied to just the right consistency and served in white porcelain cups – with a sprig of chervil, tarragon or parsley on top.

2½ lbs. lean beef, shoulder or
    bottom round
1 lb. marrow bone
2 lbs. veal shanks
14 cups cold water
2 large onions stuck with 3 cloves
3 carrots, cut up
2 stalks celery with leaves
2 to 3 leeks
1½ tbsp. salt
6 peppercorns
2 sprigs parsley
¼ tsp. thyme
1 clove garlic, whole
1 bay leaf
2 egg whites
2 crushed egg shells
2 cans tomato sauce
2 tbsp. finely chopped onion
½ tsp. basil

Place in soup kettle the beef, marrow bone, veal shanks, and water. Bring to a boil. Simmer for 5 minutes and skim. Cover and simmer over low heat for one hour.

Add the onions with cloves, carrots, celery, the leeks washed and coarsely chopped, salt, peppercorns, parsley, thyme, garlic, and bay leaf. Cover and simmer for 4 hours. Then strain through a cheesecloth. Cool, to skim off the fat.

The meat can be used for hash or shepherd's pie. Discard the vegetables.

If you wish to clarify the consommé, reheat it in a clean saucepan and add the egg whites, beaten to a light foam, and the egg shells. Bring to a rolling boil and strain once more through three thicknesses of cheesecloth.

Pour 6 cups of this consommé into a saucepan and reserve the remainder to use as beef consommé, or freeze and keep to finish as another Madrilène when needed.

Add to the consommé the tomato sauce, onion, and basil. Simmer over medium-low heat for 20 minutes, remove from heat, and strain again through cheesecloth. (The same cheesecloth can be rinsed and used over again.) Refrigerate until cold and jellied.

Yield: 6 cups.

QUICK JELLIED MADRILÈNE

A true Madrilène is much more complicated, but this one is good, although not as delicate in flavor.

2 envelopes unflavored gelatine
½ cup cold water
2 cups tomato juice
2 cups consommé or stock
1 small onion, grated
½ cup celery leaves, minced
½ tsp. basil
1 tsp. sugar
1 tsp. coarse salt
1 tbsp. lemon juice

Soak the gelatine in the cold water for 5 minutes. Bring the remaining ingredients to a boil. Boil for 2 minutes. Remove from heat, add the gelatine while stirring, to dissolve it completely. Strain through a damp cloth. Refrigerate for the bouillon to jell.

To serve, break up the jelly with a fork, place in cups and garnish with a slice of lemon. Sprinkle with paprika. Serves 5-6.

SUMMER BORSCHT

Make this the day before you want to serve it. It looks most appetizing when served in white or pink bowls – they will enhance the soup's deep purple color.

        2 cups chopped canned beets
        1 can undiluted beef bouillon
        1 tsp. chopped green onions
        1 cup cold water
          salt and pepper, to taste
        2 tbsp. lemon juice
        ⅓ cup sour cream

Drain the beets thoroughly before chopping and reserve the liquid. Heat the beet juice, bouillon, onions, and water until boiling, then add the salt, pepper, and lemon juice and mix well. Add the chopped beets and pour into a bowl. Cool and refrigerate.

Just before serving, top each bowl of borscht with a generous portion of sour cream. Serves 4.

NO-WORK VICHYSSOISE

Peeling and cooking the onions is the only work involved. Serve it cold, topped with minced chives or grated cucumber.

        4 thickly sliced onions
        1½ cups water
        ¼ tsp. sugar
        2 cans frozen potato soup
        2 cans chicken with rice soup
        1 cup cream

Combine the onions, water, and sugar and boil over medium heat for 10 minutes. Add the potato and chicken with rice soups and heat thoroughly. Pass the soup through a food mill or sieve, then add the cream. Cover and refrigerate until ready to serve. Serves 5-6.

EMERALD VICHYSSOISE

Its lovely green color looks so cool on a hot summer day.

        1 can frozen cream of potato soup
        1 cup chicken broth
        4 green onions, chopped
        ½ package frozen spinach
        ¼ tsp. nutmeg
        ½ cup milk
        ½ cup cream
          salt and pepper, to taste

Combine in a saucepan the cream of potato soup and chicken broth (1 cup water, 1 chicken-concentrate cube). Cover and heat slowly until the soup has thawed, stirring often. Add frozen spinach and nutmeg. Simmer again until spinach has thawed. Blend. Add milk and cream. Season to taste. Serve hot or cold. Serves 4.

CUCUMBER VICHYSSOISE

This soup can be made in a blender. Hot or cold, it is delicious.

1 can (10½ oz.) frozen cream of
potato soup
½ cup milk
1 medium-sized cucumber
½ cup heavy cream or
1 cup commercial sour cream
minced fresh dill, or paprika, or
watercress (if serving cold), or
minced chives (if serving hot)

Partially thaw the can of frozen cream of potato soup. Put the chunks in the container of a blender. Cover, and mix at high speed. Add milk and the cucumber, which has been peeled, seeded, and cut into 2-inch pieces. Cover and blend for a few seconds.

Pour the mixture into a bowl and add the heavy cream or sour cream. Taste for seasoning and stir well. Refrigerate until ready to serve.

When serving cold, simply garnish with dill, paprika, or watercress. To serve hot, heat and garnish with chives. Serves 4.

ICY CUCUMBER SOUP

When cucumbers are so plentiful that you want to use them in as many ways as you can, make this superb soup. You can freeze it for the winter, but don't add the cream until serving time.

3 large peeled cucumbers, sliced
3 tbsp. butter
3 tbsp. flour
4 cups chicken broth
spurt of onion juice
½ cup whipping cream
2 tbsp. each, chopped fresh chives
and dill, or,
1-2 tsp. of each if dried

Sauté the cucumbers in the butter over low heat for about 10 minutes. Salt and pepper the flour to taste, then sift it over cucumbers. A little at a time, stir in the chicken broth and onion juice (make your own by grating an onion very finely, or by squeezing it as you would an orange.)

Simmer, covered for 15 minutes, then put in a blender or through a sieve or food mill and chill. Just before serving, stir in unwhipped cream and sprinkle chives and dill on top. Serves 4.

CHILLED TOMATO AND CUCUMBER SOUP

Quick, easy, and so refreshing.

1 can tomato soup
½ cucumber (grated)
1 soup-can water
¼ cup chopped green onions
1 tsp. Worcestershire sauce
1 tsp. salt
⅛ tsp. pepper
chopped parsley
½ cup heavy cream

To the tomato soup, add the cucumber, water, green onions, Worcestershire sauce, salt, and pepper. Chill for several hours. Strain. Add the cream. Chill. Garnish with chopped parsley. Serves 4.

HARVEST TOMATO SOUP

Few of us make our own tomato soup any more, but I still do when the tomato harvest is at its peak.

8 medium tomatoes
1 bunch of green onions, chopped
1 garlic clove, finely chopped
2 tbsp. tomato paste
4 tbsp. flour
2 cups chicken broth
1 cup light cream
2 tsp. fresh dill or 1 tsp. dried dill

Slice 6 of the tomatoes and cook over medium heat with the onions, garlic, ¼ cup of water, salt, and pepper for about 10 minutes. Add tomato paste, flour, and broth. Bring to a boil, stirring constantly.

Put in a blender or press through a sieve, then place pot in a bowl of ice or in the refrigerator to chill.

Just before serving, chop the last 2 tomatoes very finely and stir in with remaining ingredients. Serves 6.

BASIC VEGETABLE SOUP

Use a pinch of nutmeg to season spinach or broccoli and pinch of curry to season peas. You can use frozen or leftover vegetables for this useful recipe.

**10-oz. pkg. frozen, or 1-3 cups
leftover vegetables
2 tbsp. butter
1 tbsp. flour
1 tsp. salt
pinch of pepper
2½ cups milk
1 cup sour or whipping cream**

Melt the butter, add the flour, salt, and pepper and cook until golden. Add milk gradually, stirring until smooth and thickened (or put all these in a blender, then cook gently until thickened).

Cook frozen vegetables according to package directions and season to taste. Drain, put in a blender, or through a sieve or food mill, and add to sauce. If using leftovers, season to taste, add to sauce, and blend or sieve.

Chill and serve topped with a big spoonful of sour or whipped cream and a sprinkling of the same seasonings that you added to the vegetables. Serves 4.

COLD SENEGALESE

A rich, superb cold soup requiring a good chicken bouillon and rich cream. A must when you are looking for a cold gourmet soup.

**5 tbsp. butter
1 onion, coarsely chopped
1 carrot, coarsely chopped
1 stalk celery, coarsely chopped
1 tsp. curry powder
2 small cinnamon sticks
2 bay leaves
1 tsp. whole cloves
5 cups chicken bouillon
1 tbsp. tomato paste
1 tbsp. red currant jelly
3 tbsp. flour
salt and pepper, to taste
2 cups rich cream**

Melt 2 tablespoons butter in a saucepan, add the onion, carrot, and celery. Simmer over medium heat, stirring often, until the vegetables are lightly browned here and there. Stir in the curry powder until well blended. Add the cinnamon sticks, bay leaves, cloves, chicken bouillon, tomato paste, and red currant jelly. Mix well, bring to a boil, then simmer over low heat for one hour. Knead the remaining butter with the flour and add to soup, stirring fast until well blended and slightly thickened. Simmer 5 minutes. Strain. Taste for seasoning and refrigerate covered.

Just before serving, stir in the cream. Garnish with minced chives or parsley.

The part of the soup that is refrigerated can be made several days ahead of time, or frozen for several weeks. To serve, thaw and beat in the cream. Serves 8.

CHILLED SEAFOOD BISQUE

Perfect for eating in the garden on a hot sunny day.

    1 can tomato soup
    1 can milk
    1 can (4½ oz.) small shrimp
    1 can (6½ oz.) crabmeat
    ½ cup red wine
        salt and pepper, to taste
        lemon juice
        chopped chives

Beat the tomato soup and milk until smooth. Add the drained shrimps, the flaked crabmeat, and the red wine. Season to taste with salt, pepper, and lemon juice. Chill. Sprinkle with chopped chives and serve. Serves 4.

CHAPTER 3

FISH AND SHELLFISH

Have you ever tasted a delicately herbed, baked lake trout, a moist panbroiled salmon or halibut steak, a hearty fish mess, or a refreshing fish aspic? If you have, then you know how wonderful fish can be. It does not take much effort to achieve good results because to cook fish to perfection you only have to remember two things:

Fish is highly perishable, therefore the fresher the better. When purchased frozen, it is important to buy the best quality and thaw it just long enough to be able to separate the pieces.

Fish, *at no time*, should be overcooked, because it then becomes tough and dry. A good rule to remember is to cook any fish 10 minutes per inch of thickness (measured at its thickest part).

A half pound of dressed or cleaned fish, or frozen or fresh fillets will serve one.

A third of a pound of fish steaks or sticks will serve one.

How to Buy Fresh Fish

Look for the following clues:

There should be very little, if any, fishy odor.

The flesh should spring back when it is pressed and it should be attached firmly to the bones.

The eyes should be bright, transparent, and somewhat protruding.

The gills should be red and not shiny.

A fresh fillet should have a firm texture, a mild odor, and no dried-out or brownish look around the edges.

What about Shellfish?

The rules for buying and cooking shellfish are the same as for fish – the fresher the better and never overcook.

Fresh Shrimps have a firm texture and a mild odor. The shells of uncooked shrimps range in color from grayish green to a light pink. When cooked, their color changes to an all-over pinky red. The term "green shrimps" is a trade description for all uncooked shrimps.

A general rule is that one pound will serve four. Of course it depends on how big they are.

Fresh Lobster A good live lobster moves its legs and when picked up,

45

curls its tail under its body. If the tail hangs limp, the lobster is dead and should not be purchased.

Serving portions depend on the size of the lobster. One small lobster of say, one pound, will serve only one person. A larger lobster would be enough for two.

Scallops In Canada, scallops are sold already cleaned, without their beautiful symmetrical shells. Although this makes the job of preparing them a lot easier, it also makes them a lot less decorative.

Containing high levels of well balanced protein and very little fat, scallops are among our least expensive shellfish, because most of the world's catch comes from the Atlantic coast. You can buy them frozen in one-pound packages or fresh by the pound. There are two kinds of scallops – bay and sea. The sea scallop is larger and the meat is white. The bay scallop varies in color from creamy white to pale pink.

Always take care not to overcook scallops, as they will be tough and stringy instead of tender and creamy. One pound will serve six small portions.

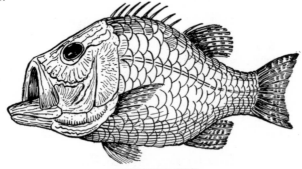

FISH FUMET

Fumet, used in haute cuisine as part of the liquid in fish sauces, or to poach fillets, or small fish, is almost a must for the French touch. A very concentrated court bouillon, it always contains fish bones, heads, or tails, or all three. It will keep several weeks refrigerated or three months frozen.

> **1½ - 2 lbs. fish trimmings**
> **(bones, heads, tails, fins)**
> **2 cups water**
> **1 bay leaf**
> **1 onion, sliced**
> **2 cups any white wine**
> **1 carrot, brushed and sliced**
> **2 celery stalks, cut in 1-inch pieces**
> **2 tbsp. chopped parsley**
> **¼ tsp. each, salt and pepper**

Bring all the ingredients to a boil in a heavy saucepan, cover, and simmer for one hour or until liquid is reduced by half. Pour into a sieve lined with cheesecloth, letting it drip through untouched, for about 30 minutes. Makes about 3 cups.

Cod

I think of cod as the old faithful. While other fish come and go according to season, cod, from the Grand Banks of Newfoundland, is always with us.

A lean, flaky fish, it is available in fillets, steaks, or sticks, and comes fresh frozen, salted, pickled, flaked, smoked, or shredded. Even cod tongues are available – a unique delicacy.

While in Canada it is the most neglected of all fish, a forgotten delight, the Europeans make interesting and tasty dishes with cod. Why don't we? I am convinced it is because we truly do not know how to cook it.

BOILED COD

This recipe, made with fresh cod, proves that it can be served as an attractive and delicious party dish.

> **3 - 5 lbs. fresh cod, in one piece**
> **1 tbsp. coarse salt**
> **8 cups cold water**
> **10 peppercorns or ½ tsp. pepper**
> **cut peel of 1 lemon**

Rinse cod and brush all over with salt. Cover and let stand for one hour in refrigerator, then place in the cold water with peppercorns and lemon peel.

Heat until water is warm, then simmer, uncovered, for 10 minutes per inch of thickness of fish or, until it flakes. When ready, remove fish from water with a perforated ladle. Set on a hot platter. Top with a few sprigs of parsley and serve with bowls of the following garnishes:

Potatoes boiled in their jackets, melted butter with grated lemon peel, to taste, finely chopped raw onions mixed with parsley, chopped hard-boiled eggs, and grated raw apples (stir in a little lemon juice so they won't darken).

Let guests take their choice of garnishes. Serves 6 - 8.

BAKED STUFFED COD

We rarely think of baking a fresh 4 to 5 lb. cod, yet it is so good. The result will surprise you.

> **4 to 5 lbs. fresh cod in one piece**
> **1 cup cracker crumbs**
> **¼ tsp. pepper**
> **1 tsp. each, salt and pepper**
> **1 small onion, minced**
> **1 tbsp. capers or 1 tsp. sweet**
> **pickles, chopped**
> **¼ cup finely chopped bacon**
> **½ cup light or rich cream**
> **5 thin slices of salt pork**

Wash the cod under running cold water. Wipe dry with a paper towel.

Combine the remaining ingredients, except the slices of salt pork. Stuff the cod with this mixture and tie it so that the stuffing will not fall out. Place the fish on a baking sheet lined with foil paper. Preheat oven to 350° F. Dredge the fish with a little flour and pour a cup of cold water in the pan. Place the salt pork on the fish and bake for 60 to 80 minutes, basting frequently. Do not let the fish get dry. Remove carefully to a hot platter. Add to pan juices ½ teaspoon curry powder and 2 tablespoons chutney or sweet relish and 1 tablespoon butter. Heat, stirring. Serve as gravy. Serves 6.

COD FILLETS WITH GRAPEFRUIT

Fresh or frozen fillets or steaks can be used. This recipe is unusual and very good.

> 6 cod fillets or steaks
> seasoned flour
> 2 tbsp. butter
> 3 tbsp. salad oil
> ¼ cup cream
> 1 large grapefruit
> 2 hard-boiled eggs
> chopped parsley

Roll the fillets or steaks in the seasoned flour. Heat the butter and salad oil in a large cast-iron frying pan. Brown the fillets over medium heat, about 10 to 12 minutes, turning only once.

In a small saucepan, heat 1 tablespoon butter, add the cream and the juice of half the grapefruit. Chop the eggs and add. Heat together, but do not boil. Add salt and pepper, to taste.

Set the fish on a hot platter and pour the sauce over it. Sprinkle with parsley.

Cut the other half of the grapefruit in two and slice thinly. Place around the fish. Serves 6.

Halibut

Halibut ranks as Canada's seventh most important fish food and it is found off both coasts. However, the most important catch is in the waters off northern British Columbia and in the Gulf of Alaska. British Columbia is the world's greatest halibut fishing grounds, an area that yields more than 60 percent of the world's annual halibut catch. The Atlantic halibut is caught off the coast of Nova Scotia and in the Gulf of St. Lawrence, as well as on the offshore banks. I would like to encourage everyone to taste and cook more often this delicately flavored fish. We can buy it fresh or frozen most of the year, but April is the best month for fresh halibut.

48

BROILED HALIBUT STEAKS AMBASSADEUR

Broiling or barbecuing are probably the tastiest methods of preparing fresh halibut in order to bring out the best flavor. Also, it is so easy to do.

> 1 small halibut steak per serving
> salt, pepper, paprika
> 1 tablespoon butter
> 1 tbsp. salad oil
> 1 tbsp. lemon or lime juice
> 1 tsp. brandy
> fresh dill or chives, minced

Wrap the steak in absorbent paper. Refrigerate for one hour. Unwrap, place on a well-oiled, shallow baking pan. Sprinkle with salt, pepper, and paprika.

Melt the butter with the salad oil, lemon, or lime juice. When boiling hot, pour over the steak. Broil 4 inches from the source of heat for 4 minutes on each side, turning only once. Place on a warm platter and pour on top the brandy mixed with dill or chives. Serve as soon as ready.

To barbecue, proceed in the same manner, doubling the butter, oil, and lemon mixture, using half to baste the steak at least twice on each side and turning it only once. The cooking time is the same.

HALIBUT BEAUFORT

Breaded baked halibut prepared in this classic way is never dry or overcooked. The garnish is most colorful.

> 6 small halibut steaks
> ½ cup butter
> 1 cup fine breadcrumbs
> 1 tsp. curry powder
> 1 egg
> 2 tbsp. water
> 1 green pepper
> 1 medium-sized onion
> 1 tbsp. salad oil
> 1 tsp. sugar
> salt and pepper, to taste

Melt the butter in an elegant, shallow baking dish. Mix the curry with the breadcrumbs. Beat the egg with the water. Dip each steak into the egg mixture, then roll lightly in the curried breadcrumbs. Dip quickly in the melted butter on both sides. Set one next to the other. Bake for 15 minutes in a preheated 400° F. oven.

In the meantime, clean the green pepper and slice it paper-thin into round rings. Slice onion thinly and break into rings. Heat the salad oil, put in the green pepper and onion rings, sprinkle with the sugar, and stir gently over medium heat for 4 to 5 minutes (just to heat through and soften lightly). Add salt and pepper to taste. Pour over cooked halibut and serve. Serves 6.

HALIBUT OYSTER BROIL

I first enjoyed this dish with a sheep farmer on Vancouver Island, sitting in his beautiful garden surrounded by flowering trees, on an April day filled with sunshine. It has become one of my favorite halibut recipes.

> 1½ to 2 lbs. halibut steak
> juice of 1 lemon
> ¼ tsp. paprika
> salt and pepper, to taste
> ½ pint oysters
> 1 tbsp. butter
> 2 tbsp. flour
> 2 tbsp. butter
> 1 cup milk
> ⅓ cup mayonnaise
> 2 tbsp. lemon juice
> ¼ cup relish
> 3 tbsp. chopped olives
> 2 green onions, minced
> 1 tsp. strong prepared mustard

Place the halibut on an oiled, shallow baking dish, if possible one that can be brought from oven to table. Mix the lemon juice with the paprika and brush the fish with it on both sides. Add salt and pepper. Place in a broiler 3 inches away from the source of heat and broil for 6 minutes. Turn, and top with the oysters, evenly distributed, over the halibut. Dot with the one tablespoon of butter and broil until the edges of the oysters ruffle. Top with hot tartar sauce and serve.

Tartar Sauce:

Make a white sauce with the flour, the 2 tablespoons of butter and the milk. When smooth and creamy, add the rest of the ingredients and season to taste. Simmer together (do not boil) for a few seconds. The sauce can also be served separately and the top of the cooked halibut sprinkled with minced chives or parsley. Serves 6.

BAKED HALIBUT CREOLE

If you are not too keen on fish, this recipe will make you like it. Halibut has a mild flavor; the topping is somewhat like Spanish sauce over eggs. Serve it with boiled, buttered, and parsleyed rice.

> 2 thin slices of salt pork or 4 slices
> of bacon
> 1 medium-sized onion, thinly sliced
> 1 halibut steak, about 1-inch thick
> salt and pepper, to taste
> ¼ tsp. curry powder
> 1 cup canned tomatoes, drained
> 1 tsp. sugar
> ¼ cup sliced black olives (optional)
> ⅓ cup breadcrumbs
> 2 tbsp. melted butter

Put half the salt pork or the bacon, cut into 1-inch pieces, in the bottom of a baking dish. Place half the onion on top, then the halibut steak. Sprinkle the fish with the salt, pepper, and curry powder. Drain the tomatoes, and mix with the sugar, olives, and remaining onions. Pour over the fish. Top with the remaining salt pork or bacon. Melt the butter, mix with the breadcrumbs. Sprinkle over the top. Bake in a 375°F. oven for 30 minutes. Serves 4.

HALIBUT FLEURETTE

The sauce in this case makes the dish. Sauce Fleurette is very popular in the south of France and deserves to be more popular here because it is so delicate and tasty. This is a perfect way to serve halibut at a buffet dinner.

6 **individual halibut steaks**
2 **tbsp. butter**
½ **cup water**
½ **cup white wine**
   salt, to taste
2 **tbsp. melted butter**
2 **tbsp. flour**
½ **cup milk**
1 **cup fish stock (from the cooked halibut)**
   salt and pepper, to taste
⅛ **tsp. nutmeg or mace**
2 **tbsp. minced parsley or chives**
1 **tbsp. lemon juice**
1 **tsp. butter**

Arrange the halibut steaks in one layer in a shallow baking dish. Pour on top the water and white wine. Sprinkle lightly with salt. Cover the dish with a sheet of buttered paper (not foil paper). Place in a preheated 475°F. oven for 15 minutes. Remove the fish from the pan with a perforated spoon. Set aside on a hot dish while making the sauce. Pass the fish stock through a sieve. Measure 1 cup and set aside.

To make the sauce, melt the 2 tablespoons of butter in a saucepan, add the flour, milk, and fish stock. Stir until creamy and smooth. Add salt and pepper, the nutmeg or mace, and the minced parsley or chives. Stir, over low heat, until well blended. Remove from heat, add the lemon juice and the teaspoon of butter. Stir until the butter melts. Pour over the fish and serve. The last bit of butter added to the sauce is called, in French cuisine, "buttering the sauce," and it does just that but it must never be put back over heat. Serves 6.

BROWN BUTTER HALIBUT

A "take-off" of the classic Eggs au Beurre Noir. Served with buttered, long-grain rice and green peas flavored with fresh mint, here is a meal to please the most demanding palate.

4 halibut steaks
½ cup milk
½ tsp. salt
¼ tsp. freshly ground pepper
grated rind of ½ a lemon
¼ cup flour
1 tbsp. butter
2 tbsp. salad oil
Brown Butter:
1 tbsp. cider vinegar
2 to 3 tbsp. butter
1 tbsp. finely minced parsley

Mix the milk with the salt, pepper, and grated lemon rind. Roll each halibut steak in the seasoned milk, then roll in the flour. Heat 1 tablespoon butter with the salad oil in a frying pan. When hot, put in the halibut steak and fry over medium heat 4 minutes on each side, turning only once. Set on a hot platter.

Brown Butter:

Add the vinegar first to the fat left in the frying pan. Set over high heat. Add the butter and stir quickly without stopping until the butter turns a nutty brown color. Pour over the halibut and serve.

FINNAN SAVORY PUDDING

All that is needed to make an elegant tasty meal with this light, soufflé-type pudding is a green salad.

1 lb. Finnan Haddie
2 slices bacon
1 tbsp. butter
2 cups mashed potatoes
salt and pepper, to taste
juice of ½ a lemon
1 small onion, minced
½ tsp. celery salt
3 tbsp. minced parsley
¼ tsp. savory
3 tbsp. butter, melted
3 eggs

Place the fish in a shallow pan. Top with the bacon and just enough water to cover the bottom of the pan. Cover and steam for 10 minutes over medium heat. Remove fish to a plate. Rub with the tablespoon of butter. Cool. This is the basic way to steam Finnan Haddie.

Flake the cooled fish and stir into the mashed potatoes. Add the salt, pepper, lemon juice, onion, celery salt, parsley, and savory. Beat until thoroughly mixed. Melt the butter and add to the mixture.

Separate the eggs. Beat the yolks until light and stir them into the fish mixture. Beat the egg whites until stiff; fold gently into the fish.

Butter a casserole or soufflé dish and pour in the mixture. Bake in a 350° F. oven for 30 to 40 minutes or until golden brown and puffy. Serves 6.

POACHED SALMON HOLLANDAISE

Halibut is as good as salmon served in this manner.

> **2 lbs. salmon in one piece**
> **⅓ cup melted butter**
> **⅓ cup dry vermouth or lemon juice**
> **salt and pepper, to taste**
> **foil**

Place the salmon on a large piece of foil. Set on a dripping pan. Bend the foil around the salmon without covering. Pour the melted butter and the vermouth or, lemon juice, over the salmon. Add salt and pepper to taste.

Bake in 350° F. oven for 40 minutes. When cooked, remove from oven. Close foil to completely cover the fish. Cool, then refrigerate for 12 hours. The juice turns into a delicious jelly that is served with the fish. Serve with Blender Mustard Hollandaise. Serves 4.

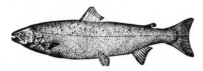

BLENDER MUSTARD HOLLANDAISE

Use your blender just for a minute and you will have perfect hollandaise. If you do not have a blender, follow your favorite recipe and add the teaspoon of mustard when sauce has cooked.

> **4 egg yolks**
> **2 tbsp. fresh lemon juice**
> **1 cup (½ lb.) butter**
> **4 tsp. very hot water**
> **½ tsp. salt**
> **few drops of Tabasco**
> **1 tsp. Dijon-type mustard**

Combine the egg yolks and lemon juice in blender, cover and blend for 10 seconds at high speed. Melt butter until it bubbles. Gradually add hot water to yolks while blending at medium speed, then add hot butter in a slow, steady stream.

Turn off blender, add remaining ingredients, cover and blend at high speed for 30 seconds. Pour into a serving dish, cover and keep at room temperature. It is best to make this early on the day it is needed rather than the day before. Yield: 2 cups.

POACHED SALMON À LA FRANÇAISE

The French use salmon steak for this colorful and tasty dish. It is then as easy to make for 2 as for 10. It is served with the classic Sauce Verte.

4 - 6 salmon steaks
1 tbsp. salad oil
juice of 1 lemon
peel of ½ lemon, grated
6 peppercorns, crushed with back
of spoon
1 tbsp. salt
1 small onion, quartered
3 - 6 sprigs parsley

Spread the oil in a frying pan (I like to use the teflon-coated type) or in a flat baking dish. Place the salmon slices next to each other, but do not overlap them. Add the lemon juice and peel, peppercorns, salt, onion, and enough hot water to just cover the fish. Cover and poach on top of the stove (in frying pan) over low heat for 10 - 20 minutes; or in a 325° F. oven (in baking dish) for the same length of time, or until the salmon flakes.

Allow the fish to cool in the liquid. Drain well and remove the skin. Arrange on a serving platter, then completely cover the fish with Sauce Verte. Serve with a cucumber salad. Serves 4 - 6.

SAUCE VERTE

If you have a blender, this sauce will be ready in minutes. If not, the ingredients will have to be chopped very finely.

½ cup green-onion tops or chives
½ cup green pepper
¼ cup parsley
½ cup spinach, uncooked
2 tbsp. lemon juice
1 cup mayonnaise

Chop the vegetables coarsely and place in blender with lemon juice. Cover and blend until they turn into a sort of mush with small bits of this and that in it. Add to the mayonnaise and mix.

Without the blender, chop the vegetables very finely and blend into the mayonnaise, crushing them to give as much color as possible to the sauce. Makes 1 ½ cups.

POACHED SALMON WITH DILL DUMPLINGS

This is country fare, most delicious and a meal in itself.

2½-3 lbs. fresh salmon
1 tbsp. salt
½ unpeeled lemon, thinly sliced
1 bay leaf

Whenever possible, choose salmon from the tail end, as it is more attractive when served.

Put the fish in lukewarm water to cover, add salt, lemon, and bay leaf. Cover and simmer for 40 to 45 minutes. Slowly cooked, the salmon will be tender and remain juicy. Uncover and cool in the broth. Remove skin and leave in broth until ready to serve. When prepared ahead of time, reheat in the broth by just bringing to the boil.

While the fish is cooking, make a tomato sauce in the following manner: Fry 1 finely chopped onion in 2 tablespoons butter. Add 2 cups tomato juice, ½ teaspoon sugar, ½ teaspoon dill seed or 1 tablespoon fresh dill, 1 tablespoon chopped parsley, salt, and pepper, to taste. Simmer for 5 minutes. Set aside.

Make Dill Dumplings in the following manner: Sift 1 cup flour with ¾ teaspoon salt and 2 teaspoons baking powder; cut in 1 teaspoon butter, 1 teaspoon lard, or 2 teaspoons butter; add ¼ cup chopped fresh dill and bind with ½ cup of milk or a little more if needed. Use just enough milk so pieces of dough can be nipped off and rolled into small balls. Roll in flour and chill for 15 minutes to 2 hours in the refrigerator. This will make 9 to 12 dumplings, depending on their size. Bring the sauce to a boil, drop in the dumplings, cover tightly, and simmer for 12 minutes. Place the dumplings around the salmon on a hot platter, top with the remaining sauce, and sprinkle with chopped dill or parsley. Serves 6 - 7.

HOT SALMON MOUSSE

This is a very popular entrée before a light or cold main course. If you like, serve it with a cold cucumber sauce, flavored with dill. The contrast of hot and cold is very pleasant.

1 16-oz. can sockeye salmon or,
1½ lbs. fresh poached salmon
¾ tsp. salt
¼ tsp. pepper
juice and grated peel of ½ a
lemon
1 tsp. Worcestershire sauce
2 green onions, very finely chopped
3 egg whites
1 cup light or heavy cream

Remove the skin from the fish, crush bones with a fork, and pass salmon through a food mill, large mesh sieve, or food chopper. Add seasonings and green onions and stir until thoroughly mixed.

Add unbeaten egg whites, one at a time, beating hard after each addition, then gradually mix in cream. Pour into a well oiled, 1½-quart fish mold, or any mold of your choice. Place in a pan of water and bake in a 375°F. oven, 40 - 50 minutes.

Let mold rest 5 minutes, then unmold onto a hot platter. Serves 4.

To make the cucumber sauce, shred 1 unpeeled medium cucumber, place in a sieve and let drain. When ready to serve, whip ½ cup of heavy cream, add cucumber, ½ tsp. of salt, a pinch of cayenne, and juice of ½ a lemon. Serve cold in a sauceboat.

SOLE AMANDINE

One of the best known delights of the French cuisine, this is easy to make and so versatile. (Halibut can be used instead of sole.) It is important that it be cooked just before serving – it cannot be made ahead of time.

    4-6 fillets of sole
    5 tbsp. butter (unsalted, if
      possible)
    1 tbsp. salad oil
    ⅓ cup slivered blanched almonds
      juice of ½ a lemon
      chopped parsley
      lemon wedges

If using frozen fillets, thaw just enough to separate. Season fillets with salt and pepper, then heat butter in a heavy metal frying pan, add oil and cook until it turns a nutty color.

Place as much fish in the pan as will comfortably fit and cook over medium heat, 3 minutes per side, turning once only. When done, transfer to a warm platter and set aside in a warm place. In the remaining butter, cook almonds until golden, stirring constantly, and pour over fish. Swirl lemon juice in the pan, pour over, then garnish with parsley and lemon wedges. Serves 4 - 6.

FILLETS OF SOLE CHABLIS

Chablis is a white wine from Burgundy and it is perfect with sole. However, you can use any dry white wine or even a dry cider.

    4 fillets of sole of equal size
    3 tbsp. butter
    2 green onions, minced
    1 cup Chablis
    2 tbsp. flour
    1 cup light cream
      juice of ½ a lemon

Stretch each fillet on absorbent paper and pat it dry. Melt 1 tablespoon of the butter in an ovenproof dish or frying pan, add green onions, and sauté lightly. Remove from pan. Put fillets in the pan, one next to the other. Sprinkle green onions on top. Pour the wine over the fillets and place uncovered in a 350° F. oven. Poach for 15 minutes, then remove fillets with a slotted spatula to a hot platter. Place pan over direct heat and boil until wine is reduced by half, then lower heat to medium.

Meanwhile, blend the remaining butter and the flour into a ball. Add cream and lemon juice, but do not mix. Pour into reduced wine and stir with a spoon or beat with a wire whisk until sauce is smooth and creamy. Add salt and pepper to taste and pour the boiling hot sauce over the fish. Serves 4.

SOLE BERCY

This one tops my list of favorites for its simplicity. The different possible combinations of ingredients give each variation of this dish a special finish.

2 **French shallots or 4 green onions**
¼ **cup chopped fresh parsley or 1**
 tbsp. dried parsley
¼ **cup white wine**
¼ **cup fish fumet or clam juice**
1-2 **lbs. fillets of sole**
 juice of ½ a lemon
3 **tbsp. butter, salted or unsalted**
 finely chopped parsley

Sprinkle the shallots or onions and the parsley over the bottom of a generously buttered shallow baking dish, then add wine and fumet, or clam juice. Lightly salt and pepper both sides of the fillets, and lay them over ingredients in baking dish (they can be placed side by side, slightly overlapping, or folded in three). Sprinkle with lemon juice and dot with butter.

Cook uncovered in a 350°F oven for 20 minutes, basting twice with pan liquid. Then broil a few seconds to brown slightly. Good surrounded by small boiled potatoes. Garnish with parsley and serve immediately. Serves 6.

FISH IN FOIL

This method works best with filleted fish and the results will be good on an oven grill, barbecue, or campfire.

Fish fillet of your choice
For every 2 lbs. of fillets:
¼ **cup white wine or water**
 juice of ½ a lemon
1 **tsp. butter**
¼ **tsp. salt**

Bring all ingredients, except fish, to a boil and let cool. Place fillets in a bowl, pour cooled mixture over them, cover and let stand for one hour. Wrap each fillet in heavy-duty foil, retaining as much dressing as possible on each. Use a double thickness of foil, if fillets are to be cooked directly on coals.

Place wrapped packages on oven grill, barbecue or coals, and cook them for 12 - 18 minutes, depending on their thickness. A one-inch thick fillet takes 12 minutes, so cook the others accordingly. Serve piping hot in individual packages.

FISH FILLETS BONNE FEMME

Fresh or frozen fillets of a fish of your choice can be prepared in this classic French way.

2½-3 lbs. fillets
2 tsp. salt
¼ tsp. pepper
3 tbsp. butter
2 cloves garlic, minced
1 medium-sized onion, cut into thin
    rings
3 green onions, chopped
½-1 lb. fresh mushrooms, cut in four
1 cup dry white wine
½ cup rich cream

Wipe the fish, sprinkle with salt and pepper. Melt the butter in a large frying pan, add the garlic, onion, green onions, and half the mushrooms. Sauté over high heat until soft, but not browned.

Place the fillets over this mixture.

Place the remaining mushrooms on the fillets and pour the wine over all. Cover the pan and simmer over low heat until fish is tender, usually 6 to 8 minutes. Gently move the fish to a hot platter. Take most of the mushrooms out with a perforated spoon and arrange them on top and around the fish.

Whip the cream until fairly thick, then quickly fold the pan juices into it and pour over the fish. Serve at once. Serves 6.

POACHED GREEN FISH

Green is for the generous coating of parsley that must cover the cooked fillets. This is a classic of the German cuisine.

2 lbs. fresh or frozen fish fillets
5 cups boiling water
3 onions, thinly sliced
1 bay leaf
1 tbsp. fresh dill or 1 tsp. dill seeds
¼ tsp. each, thyme and peppercorns
2 tbsp. butter
1 tbsp. flour
2 tbsp. fine dry breadcrumbs
½ cup finely chopped parsley

Cut each fresh or partially thawed fillet into individual portions. Place in a saucepan and cover with the boiling water. Add onions, bay leaf, dill, thyme, peppercorns, and 1 tbsp. of the butter. Bring to a boil, take pan off heat and cover – the heat of the water will cook the fish.

Melt remaining butter, mix in flour, add breadcrumbs, and 1 cup of the fish stock. Simmer, stirring constantly, until creamy and smooth. Pour into a warm serving platter, place cooked fish on top and completely cover with the parsley. Serves 6. (The leftover fish stock can be frozen and used as the liquid in any fish sauce.)

MOUNTAIN RAINBOW TROUT

This recipe works equally well with small lake trout or any fresh or frozen trout, available individually, or in 10-ounce packages. Enhance the flavor of the crisp corn-coated trout even more with a squeeze of fresh lemon juice.

⅔ **cup yellow cornmeal**
¼ **cup all-purpose flour**
2 **tsp. salt**
½ **tsp. paprika**
6 **large fresh or frozen trout**

Combine cornmeal, flour, salt, and paprika; coat fish. In a frying pan, heat a little cooking oil over hot coals for about 10 minutes. Cook fish until lightly browned on one side (about 4 minutes), turn and brown other side, also about 4 minutes. Cook until fish flakes easily when tested with a fork. Take care not to overcook. Serves 6.

POACHED TROUT, CLAM DRESSING

Many women have fresh trout brought to them by their husbands. Here is a good way to prepare the surplus because trout will keep in the refrigerator for 3 to 5 days. Frozen fillets of sole sliced in ½-inch blocks can replace the trout.

2 **tbsp. salad oil**
1-2 **lbs. fresh trout, whole or filleted**
1 **tsp. salt**
chopped parsley or dill, to taste
juice of 1 lemon
5-oz. **can baby clams**
¼ **tsp. marjoram or thyme**
12-15 **stuffed olives, sliced**

Pour the oil into a baking dish and, without overlapping the pieces, place the whole or filleted trout in it. Sprinkle with the salt, parsley or dill, and lemon juice.

Drain the clams and pour their juice over the fish. Sprinkle with the marjoram or thyme and cover the dish with a lid or foil. Poach at 375°F. for about 25 minutes.

Cool, then drain off the juice carefully without disturbing the fish. Refrigerate the fish, broth and clams separately.

When ready to serve, mix together the reserved clams and sliced olives. Add the broth, stir and taste for seasoning. Pour the dressing over the fish and serve with a bowl of radishes and tomato slices. Serves 4 - 5.

TROUT MEUNIÈRE

Another French specialty, one that is very popular with men as a lunch dish. Although better with fresh trout, it is also very good prepared with frozen speckled trout.

2 lbs. fresh or frozen trout
4 tbsp. flour
½ tsp. salt
¼ tsp. pepper
⅛ tsp. thyme
½ tsp. paprika
1 tbsp. butter
    juice of ½ lemon
1 tbsp. finely chopped parsley

Thaw frozen trout or wash fresh trout thoroughly. Using scissors, trim fins close to the skin, accentuating the tail by cutting it into a V-shape to make two distinct points. Roll fish in a mixture of flour and seasonings.

Heat oil and 2 tbsp. of the butter in a heavy frying pan, and cook fish over medium heat for about 6 minutes per side turning once only, until golden brown. Place on a hot serving dish and keep warm. Wipe frying pan with paper towels, then add remaining butter and cook over medium heat until nutty brown. Add lemon juice, salt, and pepper to taste. Pour over fish while still foaming, sprinkle parsley on top, and serve immediately. Serves 4.

POTTED TROUT

Since all supermarkets sell these delicious little trout, frozen two to a package, this recipe is not as exotic as it sounds. But it is just right for two gourmands, and it can be prepared ahead of time.

2 small trout, fresh or frozen
¼ cup all-purpose flour
1 tsp. butter
2 tbsp. salad oil
    pinch of curry powder
    salt and pepper, to taste
    butter

If using frozen fish, thaw according to package directions. Roll each trout in the flour and melt butter over high heat in a large cast-iron frying pan. Add oil to the pan and, when very hot, add curry. Stir with a fork, then add the trout.

Lower heat to medium and fry trout for 5 minutes on each side, turning once only. Season, set on a dish and let cool a bit. Then carefully lift the flesh off the bones and place it in a small dish, either in one piece, or cut into four.

Melt some butter and pour over fillets until they are well covered. (Using a small dish is more economical since only the top needs to be covered with butter.) Cover and refrigerate. It will keep 8 to 10 days.

Serve the trout cold with a basket of toast and a bottle of chutney. Spread the trout butter on the toast and top with a bit of chutney. Serves 2.

STUFFED STRIPED BASS

Striped bass is a seawater autumn fish. Any other 3-lb. fish can replace the bass in this recipe. My favorite wine to cook and serve with this is a Muscadet.

1 **2 to 3 lb. bass**
4 **green onions, chopped**
2 **medium-sized tomatoes, chopped**
⅓ **cup butter**
½ **lb. finely chopped fresh mushrooms**
2 **tbsp. parsley, chopped**
¼ **tsp. basil**
1½ **cups fresh breadcrumbs**
1 **tsp. salt**
½ **teaspoon pepper**
2 **tbsp. lemon juice**
1 **cup dry white wine or water**

Preheat oven to 350°F. Dry fish well, inside and out, with paper towels.

Peel, seed, and chop the tomatoes.

Melt half the butter in a frying pan, add the onions and stir over medium heat until limp, but not browned. Add the mushrooms and cook, stirring for 2 minutes over high heat. Add the chopped tomatoes and simmer for 5 minutes. Add the parsley, breadcrumbs, basil, salt, and pepper. Mix thoroughly. Stuff fish with this mixture. Sew closed or tie with a metal pin.

Place fish in a greased shallow baking pan and sprinkle with the lemon juice and wine. Dot with remaining butter. Bake according to thickness, basting occasionally with the pan juices. It should take from 30 to 40 minutes. Serve hot, garnished with lemon wedges and sprinkled with chopped chives. With this method of cooking, the fish will brown on top and poach underneath. Serves 6.

TARTAR SAUCE

This sauce is the classic accompaniment to fried and baked fish, but it is also good with fried mushrooms.

1 **cup mayonnaise**
2 **tbsp. finely chopped sour pickles**
1 **tbsp. capers**
1 **small onion, finely chopped**
3 **sprigs parsley, chopped**

Mix ingredients and chill at least 3 hours. Excellent served in a cup of crisp lettuce leaves. Yield: 1 cup.

EGG AND LEMON SAUCE

Here is a perfect sauce for any type of fish. The Greeks know this as *avgolemono*.

3 whole eggs
1 cup lukewarm water or fish stock
1 tbsp. cornstarch
juice of 1 lemon

Beat the eggs until they are well blended and frothy. Add liquid and cornstarch mixed with lemon juice. Beat well, then stir constantly over low heat until mixture has thickened slightly and is smooth (do not boil it). Yield: 1 cup.

FISH SOUFFLÉ

This is a French chef's recipe and no one can tell that it is made with leftover fish. You can use any type of fish, even cod, but do try it sometime with leftover fresh salmon.

1 cup cooked or canned fish,
shredded
3 tbsp. raw carrots, finely shredded
1 tbsp. parsley, minced
3 tbsp. butter
3 tbsp. flour
1 tsp. salt
1 cup milk
3 egg yolks, beaten
1 tsp. lemon juice
3 egg whites, beaten stiff
butter
lemon juice

Mix together the fish, carrots and parsley. Make a white sauce with the butter, flour, salt, and milk, stirring constantly until it is creamy and smooth.

Remove the white sauce from the heat and add the fish mixture, stirring until thoroughly blended. Beat the egg yolks until light and beat into the sauce. Add the lemon juice, then fold in the beaten egg whites.

Pour into an unbuttered 1½-quart soufflé or baking dish and set in a pan containing 1 inch of hot water.

Bake in a pre-heated 350° F. oven, for 45 minutes or until well puffed and golden brown. Serve without delay with a hot lemon butter sauce, made by heating together an equal quantity of butter and lemon juice.

MOUSSE MOUSSELINE

Even though made with leftovers, this delicate mousse makes an attractive and tasty buffet or luncheon dish.

2 cups cooked fish fillets
1 envelope unflavored gelatine
1 cup boiling water or clam juice
2 tablespoons fresh lemon juice
¼ tsp. salt
½ cup mayonnaise
1 tsp. Dijon mustard
2 green onions, finely chopped
½ cup chopped celery
½ cup heavy cream, whipped

Flake the fish and set aside. Pour gelatine over ½ cup of cold water, let stand 5 minutes, then dissolve in the boiling water or clam juice. Let cool, add lemon juice and salt, and refrigerate until it has the consistency of unbeaten egg whites.

Mix mayonnaise with mustard, green onions, and celery. Add flaked fish and combine with gelatine mixture. Fold in whipped cream.

Pour into an oiled 1½-quart mold and refrigerate until firm (it may take up to 6 hours). Unmold onto shredded lettuce. Serves 6.

TUNA LUNCHEON SALAD

One of my nicest salads, I learned to make it from a great French chef, Chef Mondage of Chailly-en-Bière, near the Forest of Fontainebleau, where my husband used to go riding. Its distinction is the seasoning of the salad, a plain dressing, and a topping of Mayonnaise Anglaise, as he used to call it, which is simply an excellent boiled dressing.

1 7-oz. can Albacore tuna
1¼ cups finely diced celery
½ cup cooked green peas
½ cup cooked diced carrots
3 tbsp. salad oil
1 tbsp. cider vinegar
¼ tsp. dry mustard
a pinch of curry powder
½ tsp. salt
pinch of sugar

Place the tuna in a bowl and break into large flakes. Add the celery, green peas, and carrots. The quantity and type of vegetable can be varied to suit your taste; fresh, cooked, or canned vegetables can be used. Then add the salad oil, vinegar, dry mustard, curry powder, salt, and sugar. Toss together lightly. Refrigerate.

Dressing:

Measure 2½ tablespoons of butter in the top of a double boiler. Stir in ½ teaspoon dry mustard, ½ teaspoon salt, 2 teaspoons sugar, and 2 teaspoons cornstarch. Beat and add 1 egg. Mix well and stir in ¾ cup light cream. Cook and stir over hot water until the mixture becomes creamy and all the starchy texture has gone. It should have the consistency of thick heavy cream. Refrigerate until cold.

To serve the salad, heap portions into cups of lettuce. Top with a teaspoon of cooked dressing. Put the rest in a bowl to serve with the salad. Serves 4 to 6.

TUNA FISH FLORENTINE

The classic recipe of this gourmet dish is made with fresh poached fillets of sole, set on a bed of spinach, and topped with a special sauce and cheese. It is much quicker and less costly to prepare it with tuna, and just as elegant.

1 lb. fresh spinach
1 tbsp. flour
1 tsp. butter
4 tbsp. butter
4 tbsp. flour
2 cups milk
½ tsp. salt
½ cup grated Parmesan cheese
2 egg yolks, lightly beaten
¼ tsp. pepper
2 6½-oz. cans tuna

Wash the spinach and place it in a large saucepan without any water. Cover and cook over medium heat for 2 minutes, turn the spinach, cover and cook another 2 minutes. Pour into a sieve and drain off excess water. Put the spinach back into the pan. Sprinkle top with the tablespoon of flour, add the teaspoon of butter, and stir together over low heat until the spinach is creamy. Add salt and pepper to taste. Spread in a shallow, well buttered baking dish.

Make a white sauce with the 4 tablespoons butter, flour, and the milk. When smooth and creamy, add the salt and Parmesan cheese. Stir until well mixed. Remove from heat and add the beaten eggs and pepper, stirring all the time. Taste for seasoning. Measure ½ cup of the sauce and pour over the spinach. Top with the flaked tuna. Pour the remaining sauce on top of the tuna. Sprinkle over the top an additional tablespoon of Parmesan cheese.

Heat in a 375° F. oven until the sauce bubbles around the edges, about 15 minutes.

To glaze the top, place under the broiler for a few seconds. Tuna Florentine can be prepared ahead of time, except for the cooking, and kept refrigerated until ready to use. The cooking period may then take a few minutes more. Serves 6.

SARDINE SALAD PARISIENNE

This colorful, tasty dish can be served at luncheon or as a first course for dinner. I also like it for picnics. It is very attractive when served in a long, narrow dish.

½ cup cooked carrots, diced
1 cup cooked potatoes, diced
1 cup frozen green peas
3 tbsp. mayonnaise
2 tbsp. cream or top milk
1 green onion, finely chopped
peel of 1 orange, grated
2 hard-boiled eggs
1 can sardines

Cool the carrots and potatoes and place in separate bowls. Cook green peas according to directions on package, but drain and let cold water run on them until they are completely cooled. This will keep them firm with a bright green color. Drain thoroughly and place in a bowl.

Blend the mayonnaise with the cream or top milk, green onion, and grated orange peel. Mix each vegetable with some of the mayonnaise, Taste for seasoning. Set on a long dish in a row, placing the green peas in the middle. Slice the eggs, arrange slices on top of the vegetables. Top each egg slice with a sardine and sprinkle each sardine with a bit of chopped parsley. Garnish with lemon wedges and parsley. Serves 4 - 6.

FRESH HERRING, MARINATED

Any type of small fresh herring will do, or you can use thawed frozen smelt.

1½ lbs. small fresh herring
2 tbsp. cider vinegar
6 tbsp. salad oil
1 tsp. sugar
2 tbsp. tomato paste
1 tsp. salt
½ tsp. pepper

Clean the herring, or ask the fish dealer to do it. Wash thoroughly in cold, salted water and drain on absorbent paper. Place herring side by side in a baking dish (do not use a metal one). Stir together the rest of the ingredients and pour over the fish. Cover with a lid or foil paper and simmer over low heat for 10 minutes. Cool and refrigerate for 24 hours before serving.

These are very good with a bowl of unseasoned greens and a plate of cucumber sticks. Let each person use some of the fish liquid as a salad dressing. Serves 4.

CRAB QUICHE

I learned to make this dish while spending a few days with a fisherman's family in Covey Cove, N.S. This is my variation of his wife's lobster pie.

pie crust of your choice, thinly
rolled
1 cup mushrooms, sliced
2 tbsp. brandy or lemon juice
1 cup canned crab
¼ lb. Swiss or mild cheddar cheese,
grated
3 eggs
1 tbsp. all-purpose flour
⅛ tsp. nutmeg
½ tsp. salt
1 cup cream

Line 8 2-inch aluminum tart pans with the thinly rolled pastry.
Preheat oven to 375°F.

Combine and stir the mushrooms with the brandy or lemon juice, then shred the crab, removing any hard parts. Fill each tart with alternate layers of sliced mushrooms, crab, and grated cheese.

Beat together the eggs, flour, nutmeg, salt, and cream, then pour equally over each tart. Place in a baking pan and bake for 20-30 minutes or until the custard is set and the top is golden brown. Serves 8.

If you are preparing this in advance, cool thoroughly and wrap each tart individually in a square of foil. Refrigerate or freeze. To reheat, unwrap and place in a 375°F. oven for 10 - 15 minutes.

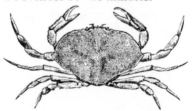

FRUIT AND SEAFOOD SALAD

Perfect for a hot evening, this can be either the first or the main course. Any mayonnaise is suitable, but the sour cream type is well worth making.

1 head of lettuce
1 lb. fresh, frozen or canned
crabmeat (about 2 cups)
1 15-oz. can sockeye salmon
2 grapefruit
1 avocado and juice of 1 lemon
(optional)
approx. 1½ cups mayonnaise
¼ cup minced fresh chives

Wash the lettuce and break off leaves. Place the leaves in ice cold water for one hour, drain, and refrigerate wrapped in absorbent paper for 1 - 2 days (the longer they sit, the crisper they will be).

To serve, arrange a bed of crisp lettuce leaves on 6 salad plates. Place a mound of crabmeat and a mound of flaked salmon in the middle of each. Peel grapefruit and cut into sections. Peel avocado and slice into thin slivers, dipping them in lemon juice to prevent discoloration.

Arrange grapefruit and avocado in radiating spokes around the seafood. Top each salad with mayonnaise and sprinkle chives over all. Serves six.

If you wish to make sour cream mayonnaise for this, beat 2 egg yolks with 1 tablespoon of dry mustard and ½ teaspoon of salt, using an electric mixer. Gradually beat in 1 cup of salad oil, adding it drop by drop until it starts to thicken, then by tablespoonfuls. When all the oil has been added and the mayonnaise is thick, mix in 2 tablespoons of fresh or bottled lemon juice.

Stir in ½ cup of commercial sour cream and keep refrigerated until ready to use – it will keep for 3 weeks. Yield: about 1½ cups.

POACHED LOBSTER TAILS

For a deluxe, cold fish platter and a special party, these should always be included.

4 frozen lobster tails, thawed
1 cup each, dry white wine and
boiling water
1½ tsp. salt

The lobster tails should total about 2¼ lbs. You can add one or two more if you wish. Split each lengthwise with a sharp knife or scissors and, if large enough, in half again to make 4 pieces. Bring to a boil with remaining ingredients, then cover immediately and remove from heat. Let stand 20 minutes, or until shells turn pink.

Drain tails from liquid, let cool, and leave at room temperature until needed. Some people prefer to remove the shells, but in the true Scandinavian manner, the cooked pieces remain in their shells.

LOBSTER CARDINAL

Whether using fresh, frozen, or even canned lobster, this dish will be spectacular and delicious. Part of the work is done early in the morning. The last touches take only a few minutes in a chafing dish.

2 tbsp. flour
¾ cup light cream
1 tsp. curry powder
½ tsp. turmeric
   salt and pepper, to taste
4 tbsp. brandy or whisky
⅔ cup tomato sauce
¼ tsp. tarragon
½ tsp. sugar
3 tbsp. butter
1 - 1½ lbs. lobster meat
1 cup long-grain rice

In the morning, blend the flour with the cream until smooth, then cook over low heat, stirring all the time until creamy. Add the curry powder, turmeric, salt, and pepper.

Beat with a whisk or a hand beater until the sauce is well blended. Pour into an attractive container. Cover with a piece of wax paper, with the paper touching the sauce to prevent a crust from forming.

On a tray, place the container of cream sauce and, in small bowls, the brandy or whisky, and the tomato sauce stirred with the tarragon and sugar. Add a wooden spoon to cook with and a medium-sized serving spoon. Get your chafing dish (or any other utensil you wish to cook with) ready to be taken out. Keep the butter and lobster refrigerated until you are ready to start cooking.

To make the rice ahead of time: boil it according to the package directions. Drain, then rinse under running cold water. Pour into a baking dish that has a cover. Place dots of butter on top of the rice. Salt and pepper lightly and cover. About 5 minutes before serving, place the dish over low heat, covered. After 5 minutes, stir with a fork. It will be hot and ready to serve.

To finish the Lobster Cardinal, melt the butter in a chafing dish over a good flame, or in an electric frying pan at 350°. Add the lobster, and stir for a few minutes to warm it up. Pour the brandy or whisky on top and warm for 2 - 4 seconds. Set a match to it and wait until the flames die down. Then add the cooked cream sauce and the tomato sauce mixture. Stir gently until everything is well mixed and hot.

This is very nice served *à la Chinoise* in small individual bowls. The rice can be served in one large bowl or in a separate bowl for each guest. Serves four.

WEST COAST SCALLOPS

This delectable way of serving scallops requires the bare minimum of cooking.

    1 lb. scallops
    1 tbsp. lemon juice
    1 cup water or white wine
    2 grapefruit
  ¼ cup melted butter
    salt and paprika, to taste
    watercress or parsley

If frozen, thaw the scallops just enough to separate them. Bring to a boil over high heat with lemon juice and water or wine, then cover and simmer over very low heat for 5 to 6 minutes. Drain and cut scallops into ¼-inch slices.

Peel the grapefruit, leaving no white skin, and cut into sections, discarding membrane. Arrange sections with scallops in 6 generously buttered scallop shells, or individual over-proof ramekins, or a shallow baking dish.

Pour melted butter evenly over the scallops and sprinkle lightly with salt and paprika. Bake in a 350°F. oven for 6 minutes, or until heated through, then sprinkle generously with chopped watercress or parsley and garnish with sprigs of either. Serves 6.

BAKED SCALLOPS

Cooking them in the oven at a high temperature ensures crispness, uses less fat, requires less attention, and eliminates frying odors.

1 lb. scallops
1 cup milk
½ tsp. salt
½ tsp. turmeric (optional)
1½ cups fine dry breadcrumbs
1 tsp. paprika
¼ cup melted butter or oil

If frozen, thaw and dry the scallops. Dip into a mixture of the milk, salt, and turmeric, then into breadcrumbs mixed with paprika. Place in a well greased baking dish, and brush each with melted butter or oil. Bake in a 500°F. oven (make sure it has reached that temperature) for no more than 8 minutes and serve immediately with Remoulade Sauce or plain mayonnaise. Serves 6.

Remoulade Sauce: Combine 1 cup of mayonnaise, 2 teaspoons of prepared French mustard, 2 small minced gherkins, 1 tablespoon each, of capers and chopped parsley, ½ teaspoon of dried tarragon, 1 small, finely chopped onion, salt, and pepper to taste. Yield: 1¼ cups.

BARBECUED SHRIMP

A 7-pound box of frozen uncooked shrimps (purchased from a wholesale fish dealer) makes an exciting barbecue for 10, at less cost than steak. Try it.

2 - 3 lbs. uncooked shrimps
⅓ cup olive oil
⅓ cup plus 1 tsp. lemon juice
1½ tsp. curry powder
1 tsp. crushed garlic or
½ tsp. garlic powder
1 tsp. salt
1 cup chutney
2 tbsp. brandy
hot bread

Rinse shrimps in cold water. If they are frozen, let them soak for 30 minutes and they will be easy to separate. Then shell and devein.

Stir together olive oil, ⅓ cup lemon juice, curry powder, garlic or garlic powder, and salt.

Add the shelled shrimps to the mixture and stir until well blended. Cover and refrigerate for 3 to 6 hours, stirring once or twice if possible. Then lift shrimps from marinade. Strain and reserve the liquid.

Adjust the grill 3 inches from prepared hot coals. Place shrimps on the grill and cook for 5 minutes without turning, but basting several times with the marinade.

Mix chutney with the remaining 1 teaspoon lemon juice and brandy. Use as a dip. Serve grilled shrimps with the dip and plenty of hot bread. Serves 4-6.

BUTTERFLY SHRIMP

Through the years, I have been asked for this recipe more often than any other. Not only shrimp, but squares of halibut or pieces of lobster can be prepared in this way. Of course, they will not "butterfly" but the succulent taste will be the same.

1 lb. raw shrimp, shelled
1 tbsp. soy sauce
1 tsp. sherry
½ tsp. salt
¼ tsp. monosodium glutamate
    thick slice of fresh ginger, peeled
    and grated
2 eggs, beaten
1½ tbsp. cornstarch
1½ tbsp. flour
    corn or peanut oil for frying

Cut shelled shrimp halfway through on inner curve and spread out to form a butterfly. The cutting is done with scissors or a sharp knife.

Mix together the soy sauce, sherry, salt, monosodium glutamate, and grated ginger. Roll shrimp in this mixture and marinate for 15 minutes to an hour. Remove from mixture and dry thoroughly with absorbent paper. Mix the eggs, cornstarch, and flour and dip each shrimp in this mixture until well coated. Fry the shrimp in 2 inches of hot oil until they are golden, and serve while hot. Serves 4.

SHRIMP VOLLARTA

Simple and elegant.

1½ lbs. fresh jumbo shrimp
    juice of 1 or 2 fresh limes
2 tsp. coarse kosher salt
2 to 3 tbsp. mild salad oil

Split the fresh shrimp in half lengthwise through the shell and tail. Rinse out dark vein. Dry shrimp on paper towels, place in flat dish, and sprinkle cut side generously with the lime juice. Sprinkle with salt. Let stand in refrigerator a couple of hours if possible.

At serving time, heat salad oil in a large heavy frying pan. Add about half the shrimp at a time; sauté until the shells are pink, no more than 2 or 3 minutes on each side. Heap onto a warm platter with lots of quartered fresh limes. Serve shrimp as a hot appetizer for 6, or as a supper entrée for three.

CHAPTER 4

MEAT

Four Ways to Tenderize Meat

Inexpensive, tasty and economical cuts of meat, such as blade and chuck roasts and steaks, stewing beef, pork shoulder, pork liver, etc. can be made fork tender by applying one of the following methods:

1. Pound thin slices of tough meat with a meat mallet to soften the fibers. Properly done, this corresponds to the "cubing" of steak.
2. Brush thin slices of meat with equal parts of mixed salad oil and lemon juice and let stand at least 30 minutes or overnight.
3. Cover large cuts of meat with buttermilk. Refrigerate overnight, then drain.
4. Let meat stand overnight in a marinade made by heating, without boiling, equal parts of red cooking wine and water with 1 sliced peeled onion, 1 peeled section of garlic (optional), and 1 teaspoon of pickling spices per pint. Use part or all of this marinade as the liquid in cooking the meat.

Beef

CUTS FOR ROASTING

The Standing Rib is the section next to the wing. It is composed of seven to eight ribs; the one referred to as the "prime rib" is cut from the first five ribs and it is the best.

The Wing Roast is cut from the loin section next to the ribs. It is triangular in shape and contains little or no tenderloin.

The Porterhouse or T-Bone Roast is cut from the loin next to the wing. It contains the T-shaped bone and most of the tenderloin or undercut.

The Sirloin Roast is cut from the area next to the porterhouse.

A rolled roast is easier to carve and sometimes more economical, but never as tasty and juicy as the prime rib roast.

The Beef Filet is expensive, tender and considered by many as the very best. It contains some tenderloin. As this cut is usually prepared for steaks, it is advisable to ask the butcher to reserve one.

RULES FOR ROASTING

No matter how perfect and tender the cut of beef you choose, it can be spoiled in the cooking. The most important rule is not to overcook a roast of beef. Fortunately, through traveling, reading, and eating, we have all become more aware of the fact that a good roast is juicier, tastier, and more tender when it is not overcooked – pink, which is medium or medium rare, is the perfect state. The meat thermometer is almost a must, unless you are among the chosen few who can cook a roast of beef to the right degree by smell and touch. With the thermometer inserted into the center of the meat, not touching fat or bone, you are assured perfect results. For pink, read 120° F., for rare, read 130° F., for medium, 140° F. For very well done (if you must), 150° F. to 160° F. When done, remove the roast to a warm platter and let it stand 10 to 15 minutes before carving.

Other things to know are:

1. Remove the roast from refrigerator 2 hours before roasting.
2. Never let the roast touch metal while roasting. Sit it on two flat bones, placed in bottom of pan (ask butcher for them), and use afterwards to make consommé.
3. A 5-to 6-pound roast needs 2 teaspoons salt, ¼ teaspoon pepper.
4. You can expect 2 large or 3 medium servings from each pound of meat.

PRIME RIB ROAST OF BEEF

A fine prime rib roast is superb. A standing rib is best if large. Above all, do not have it boned and rolled. Give yourself the luxury of a bone-in prime roast.

3 to 4 ribs of prime of beef
¼ tsp. freshly ground pepper
3 tbsp. soft butter
1 tbsp. dry mustard
2 tsp. salt

Score the fat on the top of the roast into diamond shapes. Rub the pepper on the fat. Cream together the soft butter, dry mustard, and salt. Spread it on the red part of the meat (not on the fat). Place the roast, rib-side down in the pan. Roast, uncovered and without basting in a pre-heated 350° F. oven, 15 minutes per pound for rare, 20 minutes per pound for medium or, insert thermometer into thickest part of the meat, without touching the bone. Cook according to taste.

When done, place the roast on a hot serving platter, this time resting it on its broader flesh side. Allow to stand in warm place 12 to 15 minutes before carving.

To make the gravy, place the roasting pan over direct heat, then choose which one of the three basic gravies you wish to make.

ROAST FILET OF BEEF

Wing, porterhouse, or siloin roasts can be roasted like a prime rib. The beef filet requires a slightly different treatment.

4 to 6 lb. beef filet
1 long thin slice of fat, fresh or salt
    pork
3 tbsp. butter
1 tbsp. dry mustard
    salt and pepper, to taste
½ cup diced beef suet

Place the beef filet on the long thin slice of salted or fresh pork (do not permit the filet to touch metal). Season with salt and pepper to taste. Cream together the butter and the mustard. Butter the beef filet with it. Top with the diced beef suet. Place in an oven preheated for 15 minutes at 450° F. Roast 30 to 40 minutes in all, until the thermometer registers 120° F. to 130° F., according to taste. (Beef filets vary so much in weight and quality that only a meat thermometer assures you of a perfect final result.)

To make a red-wine beef filet, proceed the same way but baste 3 to 4 times with hot red wine during the cooking period.

To Serve It Cold:

Cook only to rare or medium and let the meat cool in the dripping pan, covered with a foil paper. The beef is at its best served at room temperature rather than refrigerated.

RIB ROAST VIN ROUGE

I use a 4 to 5 lb. rib roast (the 5th to 8th rib) to make this French specialty. The gravy is superb and the meat is very tasty.

4 to 5 lb. rib roast boned, or bone
    in
¼ cup flour
4 tbsp. butter
1 cup chopped onions
½ cup coarsely grated carrots
1 clove garlic, minced
2 tbsp. warm brandy
1 cup dry red wine
2 tsp. salt
½ tsp. freshly ground pepper
1 bay leaf
½ tsp. thyme

Rub the meat all over with the flour. Heat the butter in a heavy metal frying pan or in a Dutch oven. Brown meat on all sides over medium heat. Do not rush the browning, because it is necessary to do this slowly for a lasting effect.

Remove the meat and add to the pan the onions, carrots, and garlic. Stir around over high heat until lightly browned. Place the meat on top. Remove from heat. Pour warm brandy on top. Set aflame. Add the wine, salt, pepper, bay leaf, and thyme.

Cover and place in preheated 325°F. oven for 30 minutes. Uncover and cook another 20 to 35 minutes, or to 130°F. to 140°F., according to taste.

To serve, place the roast on a hot service platter, pour a little of the gravy on top, sprinkle parsley over it. Serve the rest of the gravy in a sauceboat.

The Finishing Touches
to a Perfect Roast

Three Ways to Make Gravy

1. A creamy sauce, obtained by the addition of flour.
2. A clear sauce, made by adding a cold liquid to the fat in the pan.
3. The perfect gravy, made by adding a can of cold undiluted consommé to the hot fat in the dripping pan. Just heat and serve.

Good flour gravy has an appetizing color. To make it a rich brown, cook the flour in the fat over direct heat until the flour is well browned, which usually takes 5 to 8 minutes.

Whole wheat flour always makes a tastier and browner gravy. But if you use ordinary white flour, it is preferable to brown it in advance, keeping it handy for use when required. To brown flour, simply spread it on a flat pan and heat slowly in a 300°F. oven, as if you were making Melba toast. Stir it occasionally, until it is light brown. Pass through a sieve to remove all lumps and store in a glass jar in a cold place.

The perfect proportions for a flour gravy are 2 tablespoons of fat to 2 tablespoons of flour. If you use more than 2 tablespoons of fat, the gravy always separates and becomes greasy. Use ½ cup of liquid for each tablespoon of flour. (Whole wheat and highly browned flour have less thickening power and it is best to add an extra tablespoon of either one.)

The liquid used to make a clear gravy makes a big difference. It is not a set rule that you must use cold water. Leftover tea or coffee, tomato juice, milk, cream, wine, etc. will give a completely different flavor and color.

Simplified Brown Sauce

If you like a lot of gravy and use the fat to make the Yorkshire pudding, the English way, make this sauce, which is easy to prepare. It will keep 8 to 10 days refrigerated, 3 to 6 months frozen.

> ¼ **cup minced onion**
> ½ **tsp. sugar**
> 2 **tbsp. butter**
> 2 **tbsp. flour**
> 2 **cups canned beef consommé**
> ⅛ **tsp. pepper**
> ¼ **tsp. thyme**
> 1 **bay leaf**
> 2 **tsp. tomato paste**

Cook the onion and the sugar in the butter for 5 minutes. Stir in the flour and cook over low heat, stirring constantly until browned.

Gradually add the consommé, stirring until it reaches the boiling point. Add the pepper, thyme, bay leaf, and tomato paste. Cook over low heat for 20 minutes. Strain. Makes 1½ cups.

Madeira Sauce

An English favorite and a very elegant sauce.

> ½ **cup Madeira or port wine**
> 1 **recipe simplified brown sauce**
> 2 **tbsp. butter**

Boil the Madeira or port until reduced to 3 tablespoons.

Add the brown sauce to the reduced wine. Cover and simmer for 5 minutes. Remove from heat, add the butter and stir until it melts. Serve.

Sauce Robert

The classic sauce of French cuisine, used here to reheat quickly, thinly sliced leftover roast of beef.

> 1 **onion, minced**
> 1 **tbsp. butter**
> 1 **tbsp. salad oil**
> 1 **cup white wine**
> 1 **recipe of simplified brown sauce**
> 3 **to 4 tsp. prepared Dijon mustard**
> 3 **tbsp. soft butter**
> 3 **tbsp. parsley, minced**

Brown the onion in the 1 tablespoon butter and salad oil. Add the wine and boil over high beat until reduced to 3 or 4 tablespoons.

Heat the brown sauce and add the reduced wine. Simmer for a few moments while stirring.

Blend together the mustard, soft butter, and minced parsley. Remove the sauce from heat and add the mustard mixture. Stir until the butter melts. Taste for seasoning.

77

Canadian Yorkshire Pudding

3 eggs
1 cup milk
3 tbsp. melted butter
1 cup flour
½ tsp. salt

Preheat oven to 375°F. Grease nine 3-inch muffin cups. Beat eggs slightly in the milk and butter. Then gradually beat in flour and salt. Pour 1 teaspoon hot beef fat into each cup. Then fill muffin cups about ¾ full. Bake 40 minutes or until light to lift and golden brown. Remove from oven. Serve immediately.

English Yorkshire Pudding

2 eggs
1 cup milk
1 tsp. melted butter
1 cup flour
½ tsp. salt

Beat the eggs until light and foamy. Add the milk and the melted butter. Mix the flour and salt and stir into the egg mixture. Beat together 1 minute with a rotary beater. Let stand 1 hour. After the cooked roast has been removed from the pan, pour the batter into the fat left in the pan. Bake in a 400°F. oven, 30 to 35 minutes or until the pudding is all puffed up and golden brown. Cut in squares and place around the roast.

BLUE MONDAY POT ROAST

Moist and tender. It will brighten any blue Monday.

3 to 4 lbs. beef chuck roast
2 tsp. salt
1 tsp. thyme
2 bay leaves, broken up
¼ tsp. pepper
1 cup diced onions
1 cup diced celery
½ cup diced carrots
1 large tomato, peeled and diced
1 tbsp. cornstarch
¾ cup water
1 tsp. Worcestershire sauce

Blend together the salt, thyme, bay leaves, and pepper. Rub meat with mixture. Place in casserole or Dutch oven. Sprinkle vegetables over and around meat. Cover tightly. Bake in a preheated 300°F. oven, 2½ to 3 hours or until meat is tender. Remove meat to hot platter. Stir cornstarch, water, and Worcestershire sauce together. Add to gravy, stir until creamy and transparent. Taste for salt. Pour gravy over meat or serve separately. Serves 8.

POT ROAST BOUQUET

A bouquet of vegetables around the roast gives it its name.

**3 to 5 lb. rolled chuck or rump of
  beef
1 clove garlic, cut in two
2 tsp. salt
3 tbsp. flour
2 tbsp. fat of your choice
1 cup water
½ tsp. thyme or marjoram
6 medium potatoes, peeled
6 to 8 medium carrots, grated
6 medium onions, peeled**

Rub the meat all over with the cut clove of garlic. Sprinkle with the salt, then rub in the flour.

Brown the meat on all sides in fat over medium low heat, then place meat on a flat rack, on the bottom of a roasting pan. Add water and thyme or marjoram. Cover tightly. Simmer over low heat or bake in 350° F. oven for 1 hour per pound.

Add the vegetables around the meat in the last hour of cooking.

Thicken the gravy with flour mixed in cold water. Taste for seasoning. Serves 6.

Variation: When adding the vegetables, add 1 ¼ cups chili sauce, 2 medium onions chopped fine, 1 tsp. dill seeds, or curry powder.

MY FAVORITE POT ROAST

Lots of flavor and a tantalizing aroma.

**3 to 4 lb. round-bone chuck roast
  or bottom round
2 tbsp. soft butter or olive oil
2 tsp. salt
¼ tsp. freshly ground pepper
1 large unpeeled lemon, sliced
2 medium onions, thinly sliced
1 cup ketchup
½ tsp. tarragon or basil
¼ cup red wine or water**

Place meat in a large baking dish. Rub top with softened butter or with oil. Season with salt and pepper. Cover with slices of lemon and onion. Combine remaining ingredients and pour over meat.

Cover tightly so the meat will steam tender.

Cook in a 350° F. oven for 2 to 3 hours or until tender. Serves 6.

POT AU FEU

Pot-au-feu (or boiled beef) means a kind of homemade family soup simmered in a deep earthenware pot; essentially, it is a complete meal, composed of different meats and birds, lots of "pot vegetables" and subtle flavoring. It is regarded as one of the oldest cooking methods and is a traditional family meal; as such, it has all types of variations, and it is served around the world.

Whether it is served as Petite Marmite, or Pot-au-Feu Albigeois with dry smoked sausages, or Poule-au-Pot, or Hot Pot, or as a Provençal Aigo-Bouido filled with garlic, and so on, every country has its own. Each recipe has a special sauce to pour over the meat or vegetables, and there are many ways to warm up the leftovers – the most famous being the Miroton of Beef.

The traditional way of serving a pot-au-feu calls for large old fashioned soup plates in which meat and vegeatbles are served together, topped with the sauce. A cup of broth is often served separately.

> 3 to 5 lbs. meatless beef bones
> 2½ lbs. brisket, shank, cross-cut,
>   round, or chuck
> 1 lb. chicken giblets
> 4 qts. cold water
> 1 tbsp. coarse salt
> 4 onions, left whole
> 4 carrots, left whole
> 1 or 2 leeks, split in half (if
>   available)
> 1 cup diced celery and leaves
> 4 whole cloves
> 1 tsp. thyme
> ½ tsp. dry mustard

Ask the butcher to crack or cut the bones. Place in a large soup kettle, add the meat and the cleaned chicken giblets. Pour the cold water over all. Add the salt. Cover and bring to the boiling point over medium heat. When it boils, remove the gray scum that accumulates with a perforated spoon. Then add remaining ingredients, again bring back to the boiling point and skim with the perforated spoon. Cover and simmer over low heat for 3 to 4 hours or until the beef is tender. Remove the meat and vegetables. Serves 6-8.

To Keep the Broth:

Spread a damp cloth over a large bowl. Empty the contents of the soup kettle into the cloth. Let it drain without touching. Pour into milk bottles, cover, and refrigerate. When the consommé cools, the fat will rise to the top and harden, which prevents air from penetrating and the consommé may be kept, refrigerated, from 2 to 3 weeks. The cooled consommé is jellied. There will be 3 to 3½ quarts of consommé.

SECOND DAY POT-AU-FEU

Serve a delectable meal with the cooked meat and vegetables of the pot-au-feu accompanied by a caper, pickle, or horseradish sauce.

Caper or Sour Pickle Sauce:

> 2 tbsp. butter
> 3 tbsp. flour
> 2 cups strained broth
> 2 tbsp. capers or 3 tbsp. diced sour
>   pickles
> 1 tbsp. vinegar
>   salt and pepper, to taste
> 1 tbsp. freshly chopped parsley or
>   dill

Melt the butter, add the flour, blend and add the broth and stir until creamy over medium heat. Add the capers or sour pickles and the vinegar. Simmer for a few minutes. Season with salt and pepper. Add the parsley or dill.

Horseradish Sauce:

> ¼ cup prepared horseradish,
>   drained
> 1 tsp. sugar
> ½ tsp. French or German mustard
> ¼ tsp. salt
> 1 cup dairy sour cream

Place all the ingredients in a bowl. Beat for a minute with a rotary beater. Refrigerate until ready to serve.

To Serve:

On a large plate, place a few slices of the boiled beef, add a carrot, onion, and a bit of celery next to the meat. Have some hot boiled potatoes ready. Place one or two next to the vegetables. When using the caper or pickle sauce, pour it boiling hot over the meat and vegetables.

The horseradish sauce is best served separately, to use according to taste.

PETITE MARMITE

Called Petite (or Little), it is the grandest and most elegant of all pot-au-feu recipes. Many chic and exclusive Paris restaurants feature it as a specialty. Traditionally it is cooked and served in a special deep earthenware pot.

> ¾ lb. top round
> 1 lb. rib of beef
> 1 large marrow bone, sliced
> 10 cups cold beef or chicken broth
> 3 sets of chicken giblets
> 2 leeks or 4 onions
> 3 carrots, whole
> 1 small head of celery, cut in 4
> 1 small cabbage, cut in wedges

Wrap the top round, the rib, and the marrow bone in a cheesecloth. Place in saucepan with the cold beef broth. Bring to a rolling boil and skim.

Add the chicken giblets, the leeks split in two (the green and the white) or the whole onions, the carrots, celery, and cabbage. Bring back to a boil. Cover and simmer over very low heat for 4 hours. Taste for seasoning.

To serve, remove surplus fat. Unwrap the meat and transfer it to a hot dish. Remove the marrow from the bones and cut the meat into individual portions.

Prepare 6 slices of toasted bread, put one on each plate, spread each one with marrow, and pour some of the broth on top. Then serve a helping of meat, and vegetables on top of that. Serves 6.

Green Sauce

A classic sauce to serve with all types of pot-au-feu, especially the Petite Marmite. Will keep 6 to 8 weeks, refrigerated and covered. Leave at room temperature for a few hours before serving, as the oil will cloud when refrigerated.

> 1 small onion, grated
> 3 tbsp. parsley, chopped
> 1 tbsp. capers, chopped
> 1 clove garlic, crushed
> 1 tbsp. coarse breadcrumbs
> 4 tbsp. salad oil
> juice of ½ lemon
> salt and pepper, to taste

Place in a bowl the onion, parsley, capers, garlic, and breadcrumbs. Mash together until well blended. Add the oil and lemon juice gradually, stirring all the time until well blended. Season with salt and pepper. Yield: about 1 cup.

Steak

Whether you cook your steak over charcoal, by gas or electricity, or in a frying pan, the real problem is to know when it is done. Here are a few pointers that will help you cook a perfect steak.

1. Let the meat warm to room temperature.
2. Remove all visible excess fat and cut thick sinews from the edges.
3. Do not salt the steak. Pepper is permitted.
4. Do not place it closer than 3 inches to the flame or coals.
5. Learn the degree of cooking that suits your taste – from the color and appearance of your favorite steak when it is done to the degree you want.
6. Do not forget that you can put it back to cook if it is too rare; but when overcooked you can do nothing.
7. If the steak is sautéed, heat the butter to just below the burning point, allowing not more than a teaspoon per serving. Do not start it until you are ready to serve. If the butter is at the proper temperature, an inch-thick steak will cook rare in 4 minutes.

8. A 1½-to 2-inch steak, placed on the oven rack 3 inches from the flame, will broil rare in 8 minutes. Leave the oven door ajar when broiling.
9. Try pan frying your steak in melted steak suet for a superb flavor. Pour off the fat as it accumulates in the pan during the cooking period.

WORLD-FAMOUS STEAK AU POIVRE

Men seem to have a real fondness for this one.

> **2 lbs. sirloin or T-bone steak, 1½ inches thick**
> **¾ tsp. coarse ground peppercorns**
> **½ tbsp. coarse salt**
> **2 tbsp. butter**
> **2 tbsp. salad oil**
> **¼ cup undiluted, canned consommé**
> **½ cup red wine or brandy**

Place half the pepper and half the coarse salt on top of the steak and pound in lightly with the back of a wooden spoon. Turn and do the same on the other side. Let stand at room temperature for one to 3 hours.

To cook, heat the butter and salad oil to smoking point in a large heavy metal frying pan. Put in the steak. Sauté over high heat until seared and browned: 5 minutes on each side for rare, 7 minutes for medium rare. Lower heat slightly only if necessary during the cooking period. Place the steak on a heated serving plate. Keep warm. Add the consommé, red wine or brandy to the pan juices and stir while scraping the bottom until it just comes to a boil. Then simmer over low heat for 2 minutes. Spoon over the steak. Serve with bunches of watercress, creamed spinach, and boiled buttered rice. Serves 4.

WINNIPEG BUTTER ROAST SIRLOIN

This superb steak was served to me in Minneapolis, where they referred to it by this name. I was told that on weekends, when Canadians and Americans cross the border to shop in each other's country, the Americans always have this "good Canadian steak".

> **3 lbs. sirloin steak, 1½-inches thick**
> **½ cup butter**
> **1½ tsp. salt**
> **¼ tsp. pepper**

With half the butter, thoroughly rub a shallow dripping pan, just large enough to hold the steak (the size is important). Heat the pan in a 375° F. oven until the butter sizzles. Make sure that the steak has been at room temperature for one to 2 hours. Place the steak in the sizzling hot butter. Spread a thin layer of the remaining butter over the top. Season with salt and pepper. Bake, uncovered, 30 minutes for medium rare. Baste twice with 1 tablespoon of extra butter each time.

To serve, cut into thin slices across the grain. Pour pan juices, as they are, on top. Serve immediately. Serves 4-5.

STEAK MAITRE D'HOTEL

This one hails from Old France, but it has become a classic of the world's cuisine. Simple, but delicious.

> 1 steak for broiling, cut 1½ to
> 2-inches thick
> 4 tbsp. soft butter
> 1 tbsp. minced parsley
> ¼ tsp. dry mustard
> 1 tsp. lemon juice
> salt and pepper, to taste

Broil or barbecue steak to the degree of doneness preferred. Season with salt and pepper. Cream together the butter, mustard, lemon juice, and parsley. Shape in little balls or simply place a teaspoon over each portion of steak as soon as it is served. The butter melts from the heat of the steak and spreads its delicious flavor on top. Serves 4.

Veal

HOW TO ROAST VEAL

In roasting veal there are two important factors to remember. Veal has much less fat than other meats and, although it comes from young animals, the meat requires long, slow cooking to make it tender.

It is easy to make up the fat deficiency by the addition of fats or oil when cooking the roast.

Season the meat generously. If you wish, stuff a few garlic buds in the meat. Then spread with –

> salt and pepper, to taste
> 1 onion, thinly sliced
> 2 tbsp. butter
> 3 tbsp. shortening or other fat
> 1 tsp. dry mustard
> ½ to 1 tsp. thyme,
> tarragon, or bay leaf

Cream the butter and the fat, then blend in the dry mustard. Spread on the veal, especially on the cut part. Place the onion on top. Sprinkle with the chosen herb. Do not add water. Do not cover.

Roast in a preheated 350° F. oven, 25 minutes per pound for a whole or half leg; 20 minutes per pound for a loin; 30 minutes per pound for unrolled shoulder blade; 40 minutes per pound for a rolled shoulder. Baste 2 to 3 times during the cooking period.

Two tablespoons of catsup or tomato paste, or 1 tablespoon paprika mixed with the butter and mustard, give a deeper brown color to the finished roast and to the gravy.

THE NIGHT-BEFORE VEAL ROAST

When rolled shoulder of veal is a good buy in the late spring and early summer, try this wonderful dish. I prefer to prepare the roast the night before and refrigerate it until ready to pop into the oven.

4 to 5-lb. rolled shoulder of veal
3 tbsp. margarine
¼ tsp. basil
½ tsp. thyme
⅛ tsp. marjoram
1 tsp. salt
¼ tsp. pepper
⅛ tsp. garlic powder
1 large onion, coarsely chopped
1 tbsp. flour
juice ½ lemon

Wipe meat dry with paper towel and rub it all over with the lemon half.

Mix together all the remaining ingredients. Rub all over top and sides of veal roast. Place in the center of a large strip of heavy-duty foil. Bring top edges together lengthwise and fold over twice to seal firmly. Then wrap side loosely so there is room for juices to collect during cooking.

Place in a shallow roasting pan. Cook in a preheated 400°F. oven for 2½ hours.

To serve, open one end of foil and drain off juices. There should be about 1½ cups. Thicken with 1½ tablespoons arrowroot or cornstarch. When creamy and clear, pour into sauceboat. Serves 8 to 10.

JELLIED VEAL

4 lbs. veal neck
2 lbs. veal knuckle
1 lb. veal shank
1 onion stuck with 1 clove
1 bay leaf
1 tsp. thyme
2 to 3 carrots
2 stalks celery
1½ tbsp. salt
a few peppercorns
3 eggs, hard-boiled
juice of 1 lemon

Place in a saucepan the veal neck, knuckle and shank. Add the onion, bay leaf, thyme, carrots, and celery. Cover with cold water and bring to a boil. Boil for 5 minutes. Skim. Add the salt and peppercorns. Cover and simmer for 1½ hours or until the meat is tender.

Take the meat from the broth and remove the bones, fat, and gristle.

Chop the meat into coarse pieces. Oil and mold and cover the bottom with a layer of the chopped veal, cover with a layer of sliced hard-boiled eggs, and continue in this manner until all the veal and eggs have been used.

Skim off the fat from the cold broth. Pour the broth through a fine sieve; return to the saucepan and boil fast until it has reduced by one half. Add the lemon juice and pour over the meat. Cover and refrigerate until jellied.

VEAL MARENGO

3 lbs. veal shoulder or breast
2 tbsp. olive oil
1 cup onions, minced
1 tsp. salt
¼ tsp. pepper
2 tbsp. flour
2 cups white wine
1 lb. fresh tomatoes or
1½ cups drained canned tomatoes
½ tsp. basil
½ tsp. thyme
orange rind, approximately
3 inches by ½ inch
2 cloves garlic, crushed
½ lb. mushrooms
½ tbsp. cornstarch
1 tbsp. water
3 tbsp. chopped parsley

Cut the veal into 2-inch cubes. Heat the oil. Brown over high heat. Remove from oil.

Lower the heat. Brown the onions in another frying pan 5 to 6 minutes. While the onions are cooking, dredge the meat with the flour mixed with salt and pepper. Add to the onions and brown over medium heat for 3 to 4 minutes. Remove the meat.

Add the wine to the onions. Boil for one minute, scraping the bottom of the frying pan. Add the meat and bring back to a boil, stirring all the time.

Peel the tomatoes, remove the seeds, and cut into small pieces. Add to the meat, together with the basil, thyme, orange rind, and garlic. Season with salt and pepper to taste. Cover and simmer for one to 1½ hours or until the meat is tender.

Add the mushrooms. Simmer for 15 minutes more. Skim the excess fat from the gravy and thicken with the cornstarch blended with the cold water. Turn into a warm platter, sprinkle with parsley, and serve with boiled noodles.

FRENCH ESCALOPES

A true French cut is taken from the leg – the meat is cut on the bias, into thin slices, about ⅓-inch thick. Each piece should weigh 3 to 4 ounces at most, and should be free of fat and gristle. When the veal is young and tender, there is no need to pound it. When in doubt, flatten a little with a rolling pin. Slash the edges so that they will lie flat when cooking.

4 French-cut veal escalopes
3 tbsp. unsalted or salted butter
3 tbsp. salad oil
1 tbsp. warm water
1 small onion, minced
pinch of tarragon or thyme
4 tbsp. rich cream
salt and pepper

Heat the butter and 1½ tablespoons of the oil in a heavy enamel cast-iron frying pan. When very hot, brown the escalopes on both sides, turning only once. Season with salt and pepper. Add the warm water, cover, and simmer over low heat for 30 minutes, turning two or three times. Meanwhile, heat the rest of the oil in a frying pan, add the onion and fry quickly. At this point, as a tasty variation, ½ lb. thinly sliced fresh mushrooms can be added to the onion and quickly fried together. Add the tarragon or thyme. Simmer for 5 minutes.

When ready to serve pour onion over veal, add the cream, and bring to a quick boil. Taste for seasoning. Serve with sautéed potatoes, green beans, or carrots. Serves 4.

VEAL CASSEROLE

A veal casserole, flavored with tarragon and made creamy with a layer of shredded Swiss cheese. Here is a truly great dish.

4 tbsp. butter
6 veal escalopes
salt and pepper
¼ tsp. tarragon
1 large mild onion, thinly sliced
1 cup shredded Swiss cheese
½ cup cracker crumbs
½ cup white wine or port wine
½ cup canned beef consommé,
undiluted

Melt 2 tablespoons of the butter in a large frying pan. Brown meat on both sides over high heat. Place in a shallow baking dish, one next to the other. Salt and pepper lightly and sprinkle with the tarragon.

Cover each escalope first with a slice of onion, then cover the onion with grated cheese and top the cheese with cracker crumbs. Put a small dot of butter on top of each (use the remaining 2 tablespoons of butter). Pour half the mixed wine and consommé into the dish, letting liquid spread around the meat. Cover. Bake for 45 minutes in a preheated 350° F. oven. Pour the rest of wine consommé mixture on top. Serves 4.

MILK-FED VEAL CHOPS PRINTANIÈRE

A must when fresh asparagus and new potatoes can be teamed with milk-fed veal.

> **4 to 6 veal kidney chops, 1-inch**
> **thick**
> **2 tbsp. flour**
> **1 clove garlic, crushed**
> **½ tsp. paprika**
> **¼ tsp. thyme**
> **1 tbsp. salad oil**
> **1 tbsp. butter**
> **1 onion, cut in ¼-inch thick slices**
> **4 to 6 slices tomatoes**
> **4 to 6 thin slices of unpeeled lemon**
> **½ cup consommé**
> **½ cup white wine or**
> **¼ cup dry Vermouth**

Mix flour, garlic, paprika, and thyme. Rub into both sides of chops.

Heat oil and butter in a heavy frying pan (preferably enamel cast-iron). Brown chops slowly over medium heat on both sides, turning only once. Transfer chops to a casserole. Top each one with an onion slice, then slices of tomato and lemon.

Add consommé and wine or Vermouth to pan in which chops were browned. Bring to a boil, stirring and scraping bottom to loosen brown particles. Pour over meat. Cover tightly. Bake in a preheated 400° F. oven, for 50 to 60 minutes. Transfer meat to a hot platter. Boil gravy, uncovered over high heat, until slightly thickened, about 3 to 5 minutes. Strain over meat. Serves 4 to 6.

Pork

COATED ROAST PORK

The coating, low heat, and long cooking period, seal the juices into the pork and result in a tender tasty roast.

> **2 - 3 lbs. shoulder pork**
> **4 tbsp. soya sauce**
> **1 tbsp. sherry**
> **1 tbsp. cornstarch**
> **¼ tsp. pepper**
> **¼ tsp. monosodium glutamate**
> **2 garlic cloves, crushed**

Preheat the oven to 275° and place roast on a rack in a dripping pan.

Blend together the remaining ingredients and spread this mixture over the entire surface of the meat. Roast for 45-50 minutes per pound. The meat will then be crisp on the outside but tender and juicy on the inside. Serve either hot or cold. Serves 4-6.

PAN-FRIED PORK CHOPS

This is a basic method for pan frying pork chops, which results in moist, brown, succulent chops every time.

Heat a cast-iron frying pan and melt in it 2 to 4 pieces of pork fat removed from the chops. When enough fat has melted, put in the chops, one next to the other. Cook over medium heat for 10 minutes without turning or lifting (same time for all cuts). Turn, sprinkle with salt and pepper, and add a pinch of marjoram or sage.

Then cover the pan and cook over low heat for 10 minutes for loin chops, 20 minutes for rib chops, and 25 to 28 minutes for blade steaks or chops. When the time is up, uncover, do not turn, and raise heat as high as it can go. Brown for 2 minutes. Serve.

DEVILLED PORK CHOPS

Use rib or blade chops to prepare this tasty dish. It is delicious served with spinach and mashed potatoes.

> **6 pork chops**
> **1 onion, finely chopped**
> **3 tbsp. lemon juice**
> **1 tsp. dry mustard**
> **1 tbsp. brown sugar**
> **6 tbsp. chili sauce or catsup**
> **2 tsp. Worcestershire sauce**

Remove most of the fat from the chops. Soak the chops for one hour in a marinade made of the remaining ingredients.

Melt and brown the fat in a frying pan. Drain the chops and brown in the melted fat. When browned, add the marinade.

Cover the frying pan and simmer over low heat for one hour. Serves 6.

STUFFED PORK CHOPS

A braised type of chop, excellent even for a company dinner. Use rib pork chops.

2 tbsp. butter
2 tbsp. diced pork fat
1 small onion, diced
¼ cup chopped celery
2 cups fresh breadcrumbs
½ tsp. salt
¼ tsp. pepper
¼ tsp. sage
½ tsp. marjoram or fresh dill
4 pork chops, 1½-inches thick
2 tbsp. salad oil
½ cup apple juice or water or white wine

In a 10- or 12-inch stainless steel frying pan, melt the butter and the pork fat. Add the onion and celery, and stir over low heat for 10 minutes. Add the breadcrumbs, salt, pepper, sage, and marjoram or fresh dill. Stir until thoroughly mixed. Remove from heat.

Cut a pocket in the lean of each pork chop. Fill with the breadcrumb stuffing. Tie with skewers or wooden picks. Place in the frying pan with the salad oil. Brown well on both sides over medium heat.

Add the apple juice, water or white wine. Cover and cook over low heat, for one hour, turning only once – 20 minutes before the end of cooking. Serves 4.

PORK LIVER PÂTÉ

This homemade pâté is a delicious foie gras.

2½ lbs. pork liver
3½ lbs. minced pork
2 onions, chopped
3 cloves garlic, crushed
1 tsp. thyme
1½ tbsp. salt
2 tsp. pepper
½ cup brandy or sherry
4 eggs
½ cup flour
1 lb. salt pork, mostly fat

Put the liver through the meat chopper. Place in a bowl with the remaining ingredients, except the salt pork. If possible, beat at high speed with an electric mixer, for the more the mixture is beaten, the finer the pâté.

Slice the fat salt pork as thin as possible. Use it to line the bottom and sides of the pan. Fill the mold with the liver mixture. Cover with the remaining salt pork slices. Cover the mold with a lid or a double thickness of aluminum foil.

Place the mold in a pan half filled with boiling water. Bake for 2 hours in a 375° F. oven.

Remove from oven, let stand 25 minutes. Place a weight over the pâté, (a can, for instance) and refrigerate 12 hours or more uncovered.

SAUSAGES AND APPLES

A Canadian special. Serve with toast, for a quick nourishing lunch.

> 1 lb. sausages
> 6 medium apples, unpeeled and
>   sliced
> ¼ tsp. sage or savory
> 3 tbsp. brown sugar
> ½ tsp. cinnamon
> ¼ tsp. ground cloves

Fry the sausages in a large cast-iron frying pan. When done, remove from fat and set aside.

Slice the apples, add to all the fat remaining in the pan, sprinkle with the sage or savory, brown sugar, cinnamon, and cloves.

Stir together over medium high heat for 2 to 3 minutes. Cover and cook for 5 minutes, stirring once. Uncover, add the sausages, stir again, and simmer another 5 minutes over low heat. Serves 4 to 6.

Ham

RUM HAM

The combination of rum, oranges, and brown sugar makes a delicious glaze on the ham. Even though this takes time to cook, it requires only a little attention from you, which makes it a good dish for a party.

> 1 ham, any size
> 1 - 2 tsp. whole cloves
> 1 cup brown sugar
> 3 oranges, unpeeled
> 1½ cups rum

Wrap the ham in heavy-duty foil. Bake in a 300° oven for 35 minutes to the pound. (Any size ham can be baked this way.)

About one hour before ham is done, remove from the foil. Remove the rind with a sharp knife and score the fat. Stud with cloves. Pack brown sugar on top.

Slice unpeeled oranges. Place them in the bottom of the baking pan. Set the ham on the bed of oranges. Slowly pour rum on top.

Return the pan to the oven for one hour. Baste the ham a few times with the liquid in the pan. This makes a different and tasty dish for a buffet supper.

A 6-lb. boneless fully cooked ham will serve 8 to 10.

KITCHENER BAKED HAM

This makes a perfect buffet or cold supper pièce de résistance.

1 10 - 15 lb. tenderized ham
½ cup brown sugar
2 tsp. dry mustard
2 tbsp. rye or all-purpose flour
2 tbsp. malt vinegar
    whole cloves
1 pt. light beer or porter (dark
    brown beer)

Bake the ham in a 300° F. oven for 4 hours, uncovered. Remove from dripping pan, drain the fat accumulated in the pan. Remove the skin from the ham and put back into the dripping pan. Mix the brown sugar, dry mustard, flour, and vinegar into a paste. Score the ham in large diamonds, dot the middle of each diamond with a whole clove. Spread the paste over the top of the ham. Return to the oven for 40 minutes with the beer, then with the drippings in the bottom of the pan. Bake the last 15 minutes in a 400° F. oven. Serve hot or cold. Serves 15 - 20.

SALMIS OF HAM

A salmis in haute-cuisine is game meat or wild fowl, cooked in a very involved and highly flavored sauce. The salmis of ham takes its name from the fact that it is flavored with currant jelly and orange rind, two musts in wild-game salmis.

1 tbsp. butter
1 tbsp. hot water
⅓ cup currant jelly
    pinch of cayenne pepper
    grated rind of ½ an orange
½ cup orange juice
¼ cup dry sherry
2 cups cold cooked ham

Melt the butter in a saucepan, add the hot water, currant jelly, cayenne, orange rind, and juice. Heat and stir until the jelly has melted, add the sherry and simmer over low heat for 5 minutes. Cut the ham into little strips rather than dice. Add to sauce. Simmer again for 5 minutes. Taste for salt. Add to taste.

Serve in a ring of parsleyed rice, topped with hot green peas; or replace the rice with julienne potatoes and the peas with mashed winter squash, sprinkled with finely chopped walnuts. Serves 4.

HAM BIRAGADE

Simple ingredients turn this ham steak into a distinguished dish. Serve it with parsleyed rice and corn niblets.

        1 ham steak, ¾-inch thick
        Kitchen Bouquet
        1 tbsp. salad oil
        1 cup orange juice
        1 tbsp. butter
        ⅓ cup orange marmalade
        ¼ tsp. ginger
        1 tbsp. cornstarch

Trim any excess fat from the ham (I like to use a precooked or ready-to-serve type for this dish). Score fat along the edges. Brush all over with Kitchen Bouquet.

Heat the salad oil and brown ham steak on both sides, over medium heat. Remove to a platter and keep warm.

To the fat in the pan, add the orange juice, butter, marmalade, ginger, and cornstarch. Cook, stirring all the time, until the sauce thickens, about 5 minutes. Put the ham in the sauce, cover and simmer over medium-low heat 10 minutes more. To serve, cut into ½-inch slices across the grain. Serves 6.

HAM LOAF

Serve this delicious ham loaf hot with a mustard sauce or cold with potato salad and whipped cream horseradish sauce. For a party, bake individual loaves.

        1 lb. ground raw ham
        1½ lbs. ground fresh pork
        2 beaten eggs
        1 cup cracker crumbs
        1 cup milk
        1 tsp. dry mustard
        ¼ cup prepared horseradish
        ¼ tsp. each, salt and pepper

Place all the ingredients in a bowl, following the given order. Blend thoroughly. Pack into a buttered 9 by 5-inch loaf pan or into the 12 sections of a 3-inch muffin pan. Bake, either way, for one hour at 350°F. Sèrves 6.

Mustard Sauce

Mix 1 cup water, ½ cup brown sugar ¼ cup cider vinegar, 2 teaspoons dry mustard, ¼ teaspoon salt, a dash of cayenne. Bring to boil over medium heat, stirring often. Blend 3 tablespoons cornstarch with 3 tablespoons cold water. Add to sauce, stir until creamy and transparent. Yield: 1½ cups.

Whipped Cream Horseradish Sauce

Whip ½ cup heavy cream. Fold 1 teaspoon grated onion, 1 tablespoon well drained prepared horseradish, 1 teaspoon salt. Refrigerate until ready to serve. Yield: 1 cup.

Lamb
EASTER LEG OF LAMB

Every Easter Sunday for many years we had dinner at the home of my maternal grandmère. She had a very special way of braising a leg of lamb, which I have never found anywhere else. Try it if you like a fat-free gravy and tender moist lamb.

> 1 5- to 6-lb. leg of lamb
> 1 cup water
> 1 tbsp. butter
> 1 onion, stuck with 3 cloves
> 1 large carrot, sliced
> 2 slices of unpeeled lemon
> 2 celery stalks, diced
> 8 - 10 parsley sprigs, chopped
> 1 tsp. minced basil or oregano
> 1 tsp. salt
> ½ tsp. pepper
> 1 cup consommé (any type)
> ½ cup red wine
> ½ cup light or heavy cream
> 2 tbsp. browned flour

Place the leg of lamb in a roasting pan with the water. Cover and cook over high heat on top of the stove until the water has evaporated.

Uncover, add the butter and, still over high heat, brown the meat all over. Remove the lamb from the pan and discard all the accumulated fat from the pan.

Place in the bottom of the pan the onion, carrot, lemon slices, celery, parsley, and basil or oregano. Stir until well mixed. Place the lamb on top of these vegetables. Add salt and pepper to taste. Add the consommé.Cover and simmer over very low heat for 1½ hours.

Blend together the wine, cream, and browned flour. Pour over the lamb. Stir until well mixed. Cover and simmer for another 30 minutes.

Remove the meat to a hot platter. Strain the gravy and serve it separately. Serves 6 - 8.

ROAST LEG OF LAMB

Roasted lamb should be eaten pink, like steak.

> 4 - 5 lb. leg of lamb
> 1 tbsp. salt
> 1 tsp. pepper
> 1 tsp. basil or rosemary (optional)
> 1 tsp. sugar
> ¼ cup salad oil

Mix the salt, pepper, basil or rosemary, and sugar and rub over the lamb. Place the meat on a dripping pan, cover with wax paper, and let stand for 1 hour at room temperature.

Pour the salad oil over the lamb and roast uncovered at 375° F. for 1 hour and 15 minutes, or at 325° F. for 25 - 30 minutes per pound. Place on a hot serving dish and let stand 20 minutes in a warm place before carving. Serves 6 to 8.

BRAISED SHOULDER OF LAMB

Red wine can replace the tomato juice. A rolled shoulder of lamb is easier to carve and serve than one with a bone.

> 4 - 6 lb. shoulder of lamb
> 1 cup tomato juice
> 1 tbsp. cider vinegar
> 1 onion, finely chopped
> 1 garlic clove, halved
> 1 bay leaf
> ¼ tsp. salt
> ¼ tsp. basil
> 3 tbsp. lamb fat
> 1 tbsp. sugar

In a large bowl, combine the tomato juice, vinegar, onion, garlic, bay leaf, salt, and basil. Place the lamb in this mixture and marinate it for 12 hours.

In a heavy saucepan, melt the lamb fat (you may cut this directly from the shoulder) and brown the lamb in it. Add the marinating mixture and sugar, then cover and simmer for 2 hours or until the lamb is tender.

You may make this in the pressure cooker by proceeding in the same manner but using only ¼ cup of the marinating mixture for cooking. Cook for 30 minutes under 15-pounds of pressure.

Serve with boiled, parsleyed macaroni shells and gravy. Serves 6 to 8.

LAMB IN THE BASKET CHOP-POT

This is a specialty of Cumberland in England, and is usually made with the lamb's neck cut into chops. It is a perfect stew-in-a-casserole for a cold winter night.

> 2½ - 3 lbs. lamb in the basket
> 2 tbsp. drippings or butter
> 2 onions, finely chopped
> ½ tsp. thyme
> 4 tomatoes, peeled and chopped or
> 1 20 oz.-can tomatoes
> 1 tsp. honey or sugar
> 6 potatoes, peeled and diced
>   salt and papper, to taste
> ½ cup canned consommé or water
>   parsley, chopped

Cut the lamb into pieces of the same size and remove excess fat. Brown all the pieces in drippings or butter over high heat. Add the onions, stir for a few minutes, and pour into a casserole. Sprinkle with the thyme, top with the chopped or canned tomatoes, then pour honey or sugar on top.

Place the potatoes over everything, sprinkle with salt and pepper, and add the consommé or water. Cover and bake at 350°F. for 1½ hours. Sprinkle generously with parsley and serve with a steak sauce. Serves 6.

SHOULDER LAMB STEAK WITH CELERY SAUCE

Celery and dill are a sure flavor combination with lamb.

4 shoulder steaks, ½-inch thick
1 tbsp. fat, any kind
1 can celery soup
½ cup water
1 tsp. dried dill

Melt the fat and brown the steaks on both sides over medium heat. Add the remaining ingredients and mix thoroughly. Cover and simmer over low heat for 35 to 40 minutes, stirring 3 or 4 times during cooking. Serve with boiled rice. Serves 4.

BROILED LAMB CHOPS

Preheat the oven to broil. Sprinkle the chops with paprika. Make incisions in each one and stuff with a little lemon peel or chopped garlic. Brush with olive oil.

Broil 4 inches away from the heat and leave the oven door ajar. For 1½-inch chops, broil 8 minutes for rare, then turn for one minute. Broil 14 minutes for medium, turn for 2 minutes. Well-done chops will take 18 minutes on one side, 2 minutes on the other. For well-browned chops, place them 2 inches from the heat for the last 2 minutes of cooking before turning. Season with salt and pepper when ready to serve.

PAN-FRIED LAMB CHOPS

For the best flavor, melt 1 tablespoon of the lamb chop fat in a frying pan. You may use instead 1 tablespoon of salad oil, or half oil, half butter. Place the chops in the hot fat and cook 4 minutes over medium-high heat. Then turn them and set the heat too high for the chops to simmer, but not so high that they will burn. Cook 4 to 5 minutes, according to your taste and the thickness of the chops. Season and serve on hot plates.

PAN-FRIED LAMB CHOPS
(Without Fat)

Place a square of newspaper in the bottom of a cast-iron frying pan and heat until the paper starts to brown. Remove it, then place the chops next to one another without overlapping.

Cover the pan and cook the chops 3 minutes over high heat. Then turn them and cook, uncovered, 4 to 5 minutes over medium heat. The heat can vary slightly according to the thickness and fat content of the chops. Season and serve on hot plates.

CHAPTER 5

POULTRY

CRISP STEAM-BAKED CHICKEN

Serve it with a green salad, or with celery and carrot sticks. It has only 175 calories per quarter chicken (without the gravy).

> **1 3-lb. broiler**
> **½ tsp. salt**
> **pinch of garlic powder**
> **½ tsp. tarragon or basil**
> **¼ tsp. pepper**
> **paprika**

Quarter chicken and place in a shallow baking dish, skin-side up. Mix all ingredients except paprika and sprinkle over the chicken. Sprinkle generously with paprika. Cover, using foil if you have no lid, and bake in a 350° oven for 1½ hours or until golden. Serves 4.

MY FAVORITE BROILED CHICKEN

You will find that this dish is good when served cold, but it is even better hot.

> **1 broiler (2½ to 3 lbs.)**
> **salt and pepper**
> **3 tbsp. salad oil**
> **1 tsp. paprika**
> **½ tsp. crumbled dried tarragon,**
> **basil, or savory, or**
> **¼ tsp. ground thyme or sage**

Separate the chicken into halves with poultry shears or a pair of good kitchen scissors. Start by cutting down the back first, then turn and cut through the breast bone. Remove the backbone and the neck and use these for chicken stock. Twist the wing joints in their sockets so the pieces will lie flat.

Place the bird, skin side down, directly on the broiler pan, not on a rack. Sprinkle the top with salt and pepper, pour the salad oil on top, and sprinkle with paprika. If you happen to like herbs, sprinkle on the herb of your choice.

Place the broiler pan in the lowest part of the preheated broiler, as far as possible from the source of heat. Broil on one side for 30 minutes, then turn and baste the top with the juices in the pan. Broil on the other side for another 30 minutes, or until skin is crisp and golden brown. After 15 minutes, lower the heat if the skin is browning too rapidly.

The chicken is now ready to serve. It is so good that I never serve any type of sauce with it. I suggest only a large bowl of crisp green salad and chutney. Serves 4.

CURRIED DRUMSTICKS

These are great for a Sunday brunch because they can be prepared on Saturday. Serve them cold with a green salad and hot rolls.

> **2 lbs. drumsticks**
> **1 cup fine dry breadcrumbs**
> **1 tsp. onion salt**
> **1 tsp. garlic powder**
> **½ tsp. pepper**
> **2 tsp. curry powder**
> **1 cup mayonnaise**

Wipe the drumsticks and let stand on absorbent paper, then roll them in a mixture of the breadcrumbs and seasonings until well coated. Place on a generously buttered baking sheet without overlapping, and bake in a 400° F. oven 15 minutes to set crumbs. Coat top of each drumstick generously with mayonnaise, reduce heat to 300° F. and bake for one hour or until tender. Let cool on a cake rack and refrigerate until needed. Serves 4 to 6.

CHICKEN WINGS À LA HOUSTON

My friend Houston is a publisher and a great cook. This delicious paella, adapted from the Valencia type, is one of his specialties.

> **5 cups water**
> **1 tsp. turmeric**
> **1 large onion, chopped**
> **3 chicken bouillon cubes**
> **1 tbsp. flour**
> **½ tsp. salt**
> **12 to 24 chicken wings**
> **½ cup salad oil**
> **1 cup chopped ham or garlic**
> **sausage (optional)**
> **1 medium onion, minced**
> **2 cloves garlic, crushed**
> **1 pimiento, diced**
> **2 tomatoes, peeled and chopped**
> **2 cups uncooked long-grain rice**
> **4 cups of prepared bouillon**
> **1 can (5 oz.) small baby clams**
> **½-1 pkg. frozen green peas**

Boil together, uncovered, water, turmeric, large onion, and chicken bouillon cubes until reduced to 4 cups.

Place in a bag the chicken wings, flour, and salt (use 2 tablespoons flour for 24 wings). Brown in the hot salad oil until crisply browned. Transfer to a large casserole.

Sprinkle the chopped ham or garlic sausage over the chicken wings.

Add the onion, garlic, pimiento, and tomato to the fat remaining in the frying pan. Stir until well blended. Add rice and stir until well mixed. Add the 4 cups of reduced bouillon (do not strain), and the juice drained from the clams. Bring to a boil and simmer for 5 minutes.

Break in the frozen peas, add the clams, and pour over the chicken wings. Cover and bake 30 to 40 minutes in a 350° oven or until all liquid is absorbed and the rice well cooked. Serves 6-8.

CHICKEN TARRAGON

Use quartered broilers, quail, or Cornish hens for this unusual and delicious recipe.

**3 broilers or 12 small quail or 6
Cornish hens
1 quart buttermilk
¼ cup soft unsalted butter
1 tbsp. tarragon
salt and pepper, to taste
½ cup salad oil**

Ask the butcher to quarter the broilers or to split the Cornish hens. Small quail are left whole; larger ones are split in two. Place the prepared birds in a large non-metal bowl. Cover with the buttermilk and let soak for 4 to 6 hours. Drain well.

Cream together the butter and tarragon. Place a spoonful under each piece of bird. Set, butter-side down, on a shallow dripping pan, but do not put one piece over the other. Season lightly with salt and pepper. Pour the oil over all. Roast in a 400°F. oven for 50 minutes, turning 3 to 4 times during the cooking period. Turn off the heat and let the birds stand in the oven for 10 minutes to render their own juice. Set on a warm platter or warm chafing dish. Serve the sauce separately.

This dish can be served cold, but it should not be refrigerated. Cook it a few hours before serving. Place on the platter, cover, and leave at room temperature. Do not use the sauce unless the dish is served hot. Serves 12.

COLD BARBECUE

Cook this early in the morning and keep it at room temperature to serve at night. Hot rolls on the side are good for dipping into the tasty devilled sauce.

3 lb. broiler, cut up, or 3 lbs.
   chicken legs
4 tbsp. salad oil or shortening
1 large onion, sliced
3 tbsp. each, brown sugar
   and cider vinegar
¼ cup bottled lemon juice
1 cup tomato catsup
3 tbsp. Worcestershire sauce
1 tbsp. prepared mustard
1¼ cups water
½ cup diced celery
½ tsp. each, salt and oregano
¼ tsp. pepper

In a large frying pan, brown the chicken in the salad oil or shortening. As pieces are done, place them in a 3-quart casserole. Add the remaining ingredients to the fat in pan, bring to a boil, and pour over chicken. Cover and bake for one hour in a 350° F. oven, then let cool. Uncover and let stand until needed. Serves 4 or 5.

STUFFED BROILER BREASTS

I usually prepare these the day before the party and then reheat them. Either whole or halved Cornish hens may be substituted for the broilers.

3 small broilers, halved
1 tsp. salt
¼ tsp. pepper
½ tsp. ginger
¼ tsp. tarragon
½ lb. fresh mushrooms,
   finely chopped
1 cup breadcrumbs
⅔ cup melted butter
3 egg yolks, well beaten
½ cup fresh parsley, chopped
   peel of 1 lemon, grated
1 slice uncooked bacon, finely
   chopped
1 small garlic clove, crushed
   salt and pepper
6 tbsp. melted butter or salad oil

Preheat the oven to 300° F.

Combine the salt, pepper, ginger, and tarragon, then rub the broiler halves, inside and out, with the mixture. Set aside.

Prepare the dressing by combining the mushrooms and breadcrumbs. Pour the melted butter on top and stir until well blended. Add the egg yolks, parsley, lemon peel, bacon, and garlic, then season lightly with salt and pepper and blend thoroughly.

Cut 6 pieces of foil paper, each large enough to fit under a broiler half, and place them individually in the roasting pan. Stuff each broiler half with the prepared dressing and place, skin side up, on the foil. Lift the foil around the side of each half, but do not cover the top.

Pour 1 tablespoon of melted butter or salad oil over the skin of each broiler half, then cover and roast for 1½ hours. Serves 6.

I usually serve these chicken breasts without gravy because the stuffing keeps them quite moist. But if you prefer gravy, simply warm up 1 cup of table cream with salt, pepper, a few tablespoons of brandy or whisky, and some of the pan drippings. Mix well and pour over the chicken. Serves 6.

ORANGE GLAZED CHICKEN

If you like the tang of a sweet and sour dish, this one will please you. Serve it cold with a rice salad.

                4 lb. chicken fryer, cut up
                1 tsp. salt
                ½ tsp. garlic powder
                grated peel of 1 orange
                1 cup fresh orange juice
                ½ cup light brown sugar
                2 tbsp. melted butter
                1 tsp. dry mustard
                ¼ tsp. anise seed
                1 unpeeled navel orange

Season each chicken piece with salt, garlic powder, and orange peel. Place pieces in one layer in a roasting pan. Simmer remaining ingredients, except orange, over medium heat, stirring constantly until sugar has dissolved.

Pour sauce over chicken and, basting 3 or 4 times, bake uncovered in a 350° F. oven for about one hour, or until well browned and tender. Cut orange into thin slices and use to cover bottom of a hot service platter. Place chicken on top, pour sauce over all, and let cool. Cover and refrigerate until needed, and if any fat has risen to the top, simply lift it off with a spoon. Serves 4.

CHICKEN LIVERS AND APPLES

A new experience in texture and flavor. I often replace the chicken livers with a pound of lamb's liver cut finger size. Accompany this dish with parsleyed rice.

1 lb. chicken livers
3 tbsp. flour
1 tsp. paprika
½ tsp. each, salt and pepper
⅓ cup butter or margarine
2 tbsp. brandy
1 large onion, finely chopped
4 medium apples, cored and sliced
2 tbsp. brown sugar

Clean chicken livers and halve them. Blend flour, paprika, salt and pepper. Toss liver in mixture, until well coated.

Sauté in 4 tablespoons of the butter over high heat until brown, stirring all the time. Pour brandy on top. Stir together and transfer liver to a hot plate. To the same pan, add the onion (without any fat) and stir, over medium heat, until some of the pieces are golden. Add to liver.

Add remaining butter to pan, add apples and sugar and stir, over medium heat, until apples start to soften, about 5 minutes. Add liver and onions to apples and toss together for a few seconds. Taste for seasoning and serve. Serves 4 to 5.

CHAPTER 6

VEGETABLES AND GRAINS

New Ideas with Vegetables

Beets Cook small unpeeled beets until tender, rub off skins, cut into wedges, and serve hot or cold with sour cream blended to taste with horseradish and lemon juice or orange rind.

Broccoli Add coarsely chopped broccoli stems and small pieces of green tops to partly cooked elbow macaroni in cheese sauce. Pour in a casserole, top with grated cheese and crumbled saltines, dot with butter, and bake.

Carrots Scrape tiny carrots and cut into lengthwise quarters. Steam covered tightly in a little salted water until just tender. Drain well. Sauté in butter until lightly browned and top with melted currant jelly to taste.

Cauliflower In a small frying pan, sauté a little minced onion in butter, blend it into a thick cheese sauce with chopped cooked shrimp and seasonings. Pour over firmly cooked cauliflower flowerets. Garnish with chopped capers.

Eggplant Peel and dice eggplant, salt well, and allow to stand for one hour. Drain. Sauté in butter with grated onion and turmeric, and cook covered, until just tender. Serve hot or chilled. Delectable.

Green Beans Snap ends off fresh firm green beans, and cook in a small amount of lightly salted water until just tender. Drain and arrange neatly in an ovenproof casserole. Add cream to taste, dot liberally with butter, sprinkle with pepper, and run under broiler until bubbling.

Green Peppers Toast fork-speared peppers over an open flame until charred on all sides, rub off skins under running water. Slice thickly, and marinate in piquant vinaigrette dressing. Serve drained as antipasto or hors d'oeuvre.

Peas To any omelet, add 1 cup or more cooked peas, slivers of cooked ham, and a little grated green pepper. Cook, fold, and serve.

Red Radish Carefully scoop out radishes with vegetable peeler, leaving firm shell. Sprinkle with salt, and stuff with blended cream, blue or Cheddar cheese. It is an act of patience but well worth it!

Watercress Snip crisp watercress finely with kitchen shears. Add slivered toasted almonds, and fold into baked potato that has been scraped from jacket and whipped with butter. Return the mixture to jacket.

HOW TO COOK ASPARAGUS

The Basic Ways

There are three ways to cook asparagus.

1. Tie together, in bundles, the cleaned asparagus, using all the same size in each bundle. It can be a bundle of 3 as well as a bundle of 10. Stand the bundle upright. Pour 1½ cups boiling water over the asparagus, but add no salt. Cover with the inverted top of the double boiler and steam until the tops are tender. In about 15 minutes they are at the peak of perfection—deep green and slightly crisp.
2. Split the stalks part way, leaving at least 1 inch before the head. Spread in a large frying pan with a cover. Sprinkle with a pinch of sugar, but no salt. Pour boiling water on top to completely cover. As you pour the water, you will see the color change to a deep, vivid green. Cover the pan, boil over medium heat 5 minutes. Uncover and boil 8 to 10 minutes more. Drain. I like to remove mine with tongs. I place them on absorbent paper first on a hot platter and then transfer them to another dish or just pull out the paper. Season and serve.
3. An extravagant way, if the stalks are not used, is to cut from the stalk, tips no longer than 3 inches. Scrub each tip lightly with a soft vegetable brush under running cold water and leave the cleaned tips to soak in cold water for 10 minutes. Drain and place the tips in a perforated pan. Set over boiling water. Cover and steam 15 minutes. Season, butter, and serve. Use the stalks for a cream soup or bouillon.

HOW TO SERVE ASPARAGUS

Asparagus Amandine

Place cooked drained asparagus on a hot platter. Sauté ¼ cup slivered blanched almonds in 3 tablespoons butter until they are a light brown color. Season with salt and pepper and pour the sautéed nuts on top.

Asparagus Hollandaise

Prepare 1 cup Hollandaise Sauce for 1 to 2 pounds of cooked asparagus. Serve separately.

or Make 1 cup light white sauce: 1 tablespoon butter, 1 tablespoon flour, 1 cup milk. Beat in an egg yolk mixed with the juice of ½ to 1 lemon. This is a mock Hollandaise.

Creamed Asparagus

Place the cooked asparagus, left whole or diced, in a vegetable dish. Season lightly with salt and pepper, make a well seasoned medium white sauce, flavor to taste with lemon juice, mild grated cheese, or 1 or 2 tablespoons of mayonnaise, then pour over the asparagus. Never mix the asparagus with the sauce.

Asparagus Italian

Place cooked asparagus on a heatproof dish, and pour melted butter on top, about 2 tablespoons per pound. Sprinkle grated Parmesan on the stalks but not on the heads. Broil under direct heat for 1½ to 2 minutes and serve.

Asparagus à l'Espagnole

Place the hot cooked asparagus in a heap in the middle of a warm platter. Surround with poached eggs. Pour well flavored, thick tomato sauce over the eggs. Serve as a main course.

Asparagus au Jus

Cook asparagus, by Methods 1 or 2 and use chicken consommé instead of hot water. Transfer the cooked vegetable with tongs to a warm platter. Beat the yolk of an egg with the juice of ½ a lemon. Pour a little of the cooking juice into it; beat hard. Add to the remaining juice while beating. Season to taste and pour over the asparagus. Enough for 1 to 2 pounds.

Asparagus à la Française

Place the cooked asparagus on a hot service platter. Fan the stalk ends, but keep the heads together. Pour the following sauce on top:

Have all the ingredients at room temperature. Whip ⅔ cup cream. Add ¼ teaspoon nutmeg, 3 tablespoons melted butter and ⅓ cup grated Swiss cheese. Pile this cloudy light sauce on top of the asparagus and serve.

ASPARAGUS QUICHE

A culinary showpiece, created by a famous French chef, that is delectable to eat and a change from the type served "once too often".

>1 unbaked 9-inch pastry shell
>2 lbs. fresh asparagus
>2 cups light cream
>⅓ cup grated Parmesan cheese
>⅓ cup grated Swiss cheese
>4 eggs
>salt and pepper, to taste

Line a pie plate with pastry and bake exactly 8 minutes in a preheated 400° F. oven. Cook and drain the asparagus. Cut the top 2 inches of each spear (reserve the rest to dice and serve as salad). Stir together the cream, Parmesan and Swiss cheese, the eggs, salt, and pepper. When thoroughly mixed, pour into a pastry shell. Bake in a preheated 350° F. oven for 30 minutes or until the custard is almost set. Then take out and stick the asparagus tips upright into the quiche and return to the oven until firm, about 5 to 8 minutes. Serve as soon as ready. Serves 4 to 6.

ASPARAGUS SPRING LUNCHEON

4 slices of bread, buttered
nutmeg or curry powder
4 slices cooked ham
24 stalks of cooked asparagus
2 tbsp. butter
2 tbsp. flour
2 cups milk
salt and pepper, to taste
2 cups grated sharp cheddar cheese
2 tbsp. fresh chives or parsley,
minced

Place the crustless buttered bread on a baking sheet and toast in a 300°F. oven until brown. Sprinkle the toast with nutmeg or curry powder to taste.

Place a slice of toast in an individual shallow casserole or in the bottom of a shallow Pyrex dish. Lay a slice of ham on each piece of toast. On the ham, set 6 stalks of cooked asparagus. Sprinkle lightly with salt and pepper. Make a cream sauce with the butter, flour, and milk. When smooth and creamy, add the grated cheese and chives or parsley. Pour over the asparagus and ham. When ham and asparagus have cooled, place for 20 minutes in a preheated 300°F. oven. When everything is hot, simply brown top under direct heat. Serves 4.

GREEN BEANS REPERTOIRE

Fresh or frozen green beans usually taste better a little underdone rather than limp and overcooked. To cook ahead of time, place them in a saucepan with a pinch of sugar and pour boilding water on top. Do not cover, boil fast. Drain, place in a bowl, cover with ice cubes, and refrigerate for 2 to 12 hours. Then reheat with only the liquid that clings to them over medium heat and they will be ready to serve.

Variations:

Brown sliced almonds in butter, add a few drops of cider vinegar, and pour over the hot beans.

Sauté a handful of dry breadcrumbs in butter with a piece of garlic or a bit of minced green onion. Sprinkle over the beans.

Slice fresh mushrooms, stir them in salad oil or butter over quick heat for a few seconds, add a sprinkling of tarragon, and stir gently into cooked beans.

Add a teaspoon of prepared horseradish to melted butter. Blend into the cooked beans.

Stir a piece of butter in the cooked beans until it melts, add fresh lemon juice to taste. Place into hot service dish and sprinkle with Parmesan.

Save a cupful of stewed fresh tomatoes and blend with the cooked green beans.

Boil them with a pinch of savory. Drain, flavor with lemon juice, minced fresh dill, and butter.

Blend them with fried onions and chili sauce.

YOUNG BEETS IN SOUR CREAM

If in a hurry use well drained canned beets, but of course fresh boiled young garden beets are the best.

> **2 bunches cooked new beets**
> **3 tbsp. butter**
> **2 tbsp. lemon juice**
> **seasoned salt, to taste**
> **fresh ground pepper, to taste**
> **¼ tsp. nutmeg**
> **1 tbsp. honey**
> **minced onion, to taste**
> **½ to ¾ cup sour cream**

Peel and grate the cooked beets. Place in a saucepan, add the other ingredients. Stir over low heat until well blended and hot. Serves 6.

NEW ORLEANS CABBAGE

Full of color and flavor.

> **2 tbsp. salad oil**
> **3 cups thinly shredded cabbage**
> **1 cup thinly sliced celery**
> **1 onion, minced**
> **1 small green pepper, diced**
> **2 tomatoes, peeled and diced**
> **½ tsp. basil**
> **a pinch nutmeg**
> **¼ tsp. sugar**
> **salt and pepper**

Heat the oil in a large frying pan. Add the cabbage, celery, onion, green pepper, and tomatoes. Stir until well blended. Add the rest of the ingredients. Cover and simmer over low heat for about 15 minutes or until the vegetables are tender, stirring occasionally. Add a teaspoon of butter just before serving. (No water is required. The vegetables cook in their own juice, hence the importance of keeping the heat down.) Serves 6.

C.C.O.

My family named this great way of eating carrots. Translation: carrot, celery, onion.

> **5 medium-sized carrots**
> **1 cup diced celery**
> **1 large onion, chopped**
> **1 tbsp. butter**
> **½ tsp. sugar**
> **grated rind of ½ a lemon**

Scrape or peel the carrots. Slice thinly. Dice and chop the celery and onion. Melt the butter in a saucepan. Add the prepared vegetables, sugar, and lemon rind. Stir together over low heat until vegetables are well buttered. Cover and simmer over low heat for 10 to 15 minutes. If you keep the saucepan covered over low heat, the moisture is retained and no liquid is needed. Serve when ready. Do not drain the liquid as it is made up of the butter and natural juices of the vegetable. Serves 6.

FRESH MINT-GLAZED CARROTS

Of course, young fresh carrots are the best, but you can also use well drained canned carrots and fresh or dried mint.

> **12 young fresh carrots**
> **pinch of thyme**
> **¼ cup sugar**
> **¼ cup butter**
> **3 tbsp. fresh mint, chopped**

Wash, scrape carrots. Place in a saucepan. Add a pinch of the sugar and thyme, pour boiling water on top. Cover and boil for 10 to 15 minutes, depending on the size of the carrots. Keep them crisp. Drain and cool. This can be done ahead of time, and the carrots refrigerated and covered until ready to glaze.

In a cold frying pan place the sugar, butter, and carrots. Shake the pan over medium heat until the carrots are shiny and hot, but do not brown. Place in serving dish and sprinkle with the fresh mint. Serves 6.

CHESTER MASHED RED-AND-WHITE CARROTS

A few years ago, I spent some time vacationing in Nova Scotia. In Chester, I was served this very tasty dish made with carrots. My hostess called the parsnips "White carrots".

> **4 to 5 carrots**
> **3 parsnips**
> **½ cup hot water**
> **⅓ cup melted butter**
> **1 tbsp. lemon juice**
> **¼ cup fresh cream or sour cream**
> **grated rind of 1 lemon**
> **salt and pepper, to taste**
> **chopped parsley or chives**

Peel the carrots and the parsnips. Cut each into thick slices. Combine in a saucepan the hot water, melted butter, and lemon juice. Add the prepared vegetables. Stir until well mixed. Cover and simmer over medium low heat for 20 minutes. Strain, but reserve any remaining liquid (sometimes it all evaporates, depending on the natural water content of the vegetables). Add the cream or sour cream and lemon rind to the vegetables. Mash together, and make as smooth as possible. Season with salt and pepper. Add parsley or chives, and some of the reserved liquid, if necessary. Serve hot. Serves 6.

GOLDEN CAULIFLOWER

Cauliflower is the queen of the cabbage family and should be treated as such. To cook it perfectly, steam whenever possible. This sauce over the cauliflower gets its regal color from the turmeric.

1 cauliflower
1 tbsp. cider vinegar
1 tsp. sugar
1 cup boiling water
2 tbsp. butter
3 tbsp. lemon juice
1 tsp. turmeric
2 tsp. cornstarch
salt and pepper, to taste

Break the cauliflower into small flowerets, chop the tenderest leaves, and grate the core. Place in a saucepan, add the vinegar and sugar. (This keeps the cauliflower white.) Add the boiling water. Stir. Cover and boil for 5 to 7 minutes. Drain, reserving the water. Place the cauliflower in a hot serving dish. Mix the cornstarch with the lemon juice and add to the reserved water with the rest of the ingredients. Stir over medium heat until creamy and hot. Pour over the cauliflower and serve. Serves 4.

Corn

Our liking for corn is rooted deep in our past. How often our forefathers were saved from starvation by the corn they grew and originally obtained from the Indians! It was the staple food of the frontier towns because it was faster to start than the other grains and yielded a large harvest. Quebec and Ontario pioneers learned from the Indian women how to make lye corn or hominy; the former added it to their pea soup, the latter to a cream sauce made with bacon fat. To this day these dishes are still made and still taste good. Even the cob was turned into "good old corn pipes", and toys for the young, and the grain was often stone ground into meal or flour to be used for the ever-famous Johnny cake.

Ideally, corn on the cob should be picked, partly husked and cooked, all within 30 minutes, but this is not always possible. There is another important rule we can apply. The less time corn cooks, the better it is. Usually it is overcooked. Another caprice of corn is its preference for sugar rather than salt. Unless you cook your own garden-grown corn, which will take 10 to 20 minutes from the garden to the pot, sugar is needed to enhance and improve the flavor.

BOILED CORN ON THE COB

Remove the husks, except the last 2 or 3 layers, and the silks from each ear of corn. Trim stem and tip with a sharp knife if necessary. Bring a large pot of water to a boil with 3 tablespoons sugar and 1 cup of milk for each dozen ears of corn. Drop corn into the vigorously boiling water. Boil 3 to 5 minutes. As soon as done, remove from the water. (Standing in the water makes it watersoaked.) Set on a hot platter covered with a linen napkin. Of course, lots of soft butter, pepper and salt go with corn. If you are on a diet, beware!

ROASTED CORN

The milk and sugar treatment gives it a lovely golden color and a full flavor.

12 ears of corn
2 cups milk
¼ cup sugar

Remove all the husks and silks from the corn. Trim stems and tips. Combine the milk and sugar in a shallow dripping pan, place the corn in it. Roll around in the milk until well coated. Leave there until ready to roast.

To roast on a barbecue, place corn unwrapped on a grill high over the glowing coals and roast for 10 minutes, turning often.

To roast in an oven, preheat oven to 375°F. Set corn on the grill, place in dripping pan and roast for 20 minutes.

CORN-STUFFED GREEN PEPPERS

A natural union, as both are at their best in the early autumn. This light custardy corn filling is the best I know for green peppers.

6 green peppers of equal size
2½ cups corn cut from the cob or
1 (14 oz.) can corn kernels
4 eggs
⅔ cup heavy cream
¼ tsp. savory
¼ tsp. each, salt and pepper
pinch of nutmeg
1 cup fresh bread cubes (no crust)
3 tbsp. butter

Cut a slice off the top of each pepper. Remove seeds and membrane carefully. My mother always pared away the thin outer layer of the pepper with a sharp knife. I use a potato peeler. This is not necessary, but makes a delicate stuffed pepper that is never bitter.

Place prepared peppers upright on a shallow buttered baking disn.

To make the filling, beat eggs and cream slightly in a bowl and add the rest of the ingredients. Blend well and use to fill each green pepper. Bake 40 minutes in a preheated 325°F. oven. Sprinkle the top with paprika and serve in a nest of cooked, buttered rice. Serves 6.

BUTTER-FRIED CUCUMBERS

The first time I ate fried cucumbers was in England, served piping hot with a garnish of ice-cold Devonshire cream on the side. In Canada, I use sour cream.

2 tbsp. butter
2 medium-sized cucumbers
¼ cup flour
½ tsp. salt
½ tsp. curry powder (optional)
4 tbsp. finely chopped parsley

Peel the cucumbers and slice them ½-inch thick. Dry the slices by wrapping them in absorbent paper for a few minutes. Then shake in a bag containing the flour, salt, and curry powder.

Melt the butter in a large frying pan. Add the floured cucumber slices and fry for about 3 minutes on each side for a golden color. Do not overcook. Serve as soon as ready, sprinkled with the parsley. Serves 4.

BOILED CUCUMBERS

Tasty and elegant in their butter and caper sauce.

2 medium-sized cucumbers
½ tsp. salt
¼ tsp. sugar
1 cup boiling water
3 tbsp. butter
2 tbsp. fresh lemon juice
1 tbsp. capers
minced parsley

Peel, slice, and place cucumbers in a saucepan with salt and sugar. Add the boiling water. Boil over medium heat for 10 minutes. Drain, place in a hot vegetable dish. Pour butter sauce on top and serve.

While the cucumbers cook, melt the butter, add the lemon juice, capers, and parsley. Serves 4.

RATATOUILLE NIÇOISE

Anyone who has traveled through the south of France has enjoyed this unusual cooked vegetable salad. Equally good hot or cold it will keep 10 to 15 days refrigerated. Try it with barbecued steak or chicken.

½ cup salad oil
2 large onions, thinly sliced
2 to 3 cloves garlic, minced
1 small eggplant, peeled and diced
4 tomatoes, peeled and diced
1 small squash or zucchini, peeled
and diced
2 green peppers, cleaned and diced
½ tsp. basil
¼ tsp. thyme
salt and pepper, to taste

Heat the oil in a heavy saucepan (when possible use cast iron). Add the onions and garlic, brown quickly over high heat. Add the eggplant and the tomatoes. Mix everything together, crushing the mixture with the back of a wooden spoon. Add the squash or zucchini, and the green peppers. Mix well. Add the rest of the ingredients. Cook for 2 to 3 minutes over high heat, stirring most of the time.

Cover and simmer for one hour, over low heat, stirring once or twice. It is ready when the sauce is thick and creamy.

The ratatouille is served hot or cold, as an hors d'oeuvre, a salad, or a vegetable. When serving cold, sprinkle with the juice of ½ to 1 lemon. Taste for seasoning. Serves 6.

IRENE'S CREAMED MUSHROOMS

The onion browns in a heavy metal pan without any fat. This is an intriguing way to deal with onions; they retain all their fine flavor but none of the harshness.

> **1 onion, chopped fine**
> **½ lb. fresh mushrooms. sliced**
> **⅓ cup cold water**
> **2 tbsp. butter**
> **2 tbsp. flour**
> **½ cup sour cream**
> **salt and pepper, to taste**

Place the onion in a heavy metal frying pan without any fat. Cook over medium heat, until lightly browned. Add the mushrooms, mix well and stir together for a few minutes, add the water, and simmer for 10 minutes.

In the meantime, brown the butter in a saucepan, add the flour, and brown. Add the liquid from the mushrooms and cook, while stirring, until creamy and smooth. Pour over the mushrooms. Blend well together and add the sour cream. Heat, but do not boil. Taste for seasoning and serve. Serves 4 to 6.

GREEN PEAS À LA FRANÇAISE

This is so good that I usually double the recipe and serve it for lunch with crispy French bread and thin slices of Gouda cheese.

> **3 tbsp. butter**
> **2 white onions**
> **1 medium head lettuce**
> **2 - 3 lbs. fresh green peas**
> **½ tsp. sugar**
> **4 sprigs parsley**

Melt the butter in an electric frying pan set at 300°F. Add minced onions. Cover and simmer without browning until soft and transparent. Reserve the outer green leaves of the lettuce whole, and place the rest, shredded, on top of the onions. Shell the green peas and place on top of the lettuce. Sprinkle with the sugar and cover with reserved lettuce leaves. Cover and lower the heat to 200°F.

Cook for 25-35 minutes, depending on the size of the peas. When done, remove the lettuce leaves, season to taste, add a piece of butter, and a bit of lemon juice. Mix and garnish with the parsley. Serves 6.

FOIL-WRAPPED POTATOES FINES HERBES

If you like your baked potatoes moist, wrap them; if you like to eat the crisp crunchy skin, prepare the same way but do not wrap.

Scrub with a stiff brush potatoes of uniform size and dry. Rub all over foil. Bake in a 425°F. oven 50 to 70 minutes depending on the size. Serve with a bowl of *fines herbes* butter.

Melt 4 tablespoons of butter, add 2 tablespoons of sour cream or rich cream, a pinch of tarragon, a tablespoon of minced parsley, a finely minced green onion or chives to taste, salt, and pepper. Stir well and serve as soon as hot.

POTATOES POLONAISE

One of my husband's favorite light meals. Crisp celery or a green salad is all that is needed to make a well balanced meal. Also very nice served with roasted chicken or poached fish.

> **6 medium potatoes**
> **3 to 4 tbsp. bacon fat or salad oil**
> **2 cups cottage cheese**
> **3 tbsp. sour cream**
> **2 eggs**
> **¼ cup minced parsley**
> **salt and pepper, to taste**

Peel potatoes and slice as thinly as possible. Heat the bacon fat or oil in a large frying pan. Pour in the potatoes and stir once in a while, over medium heat, until golden brown and crisp. This will take about 15 minutes. Turn into a baking dish.

Mix together the rest of the ingredients and pour over the potatoes. Bake in a 250°F. oven for 20 to 25 minutes or until the cheese is set. Serves six.

GRILLED POTATOES

Wonderful with pan fried or grilled meat. A useful recipe because the potatoes can be boiled ahead of time.

> **6 medium-sized potatoes**
> **¼ cup melted butter or margarine**
> **¼ tsp. paprika**
> **small bowl of coarse salt**
> **pepper grinder**
> **dish of unsalted butter**

Scrub and boil the potatoes in their skins. Cool and peel. Cut them in half, lengthwise and place on a baking sheet. Brush generously each half with the melted butter mixed with the paprika. Put under direct heat, about

2 to 3 inches away from the source of heat and grill until they are golden brown. Serve as soon as ready, with the coarse salt, pepper, and unsalted butter. Serves 6.

POTATOES GRÊLÉES

A butter-fried potato, coated with coarse salt or fresh breadcrumbs. Crisp and so good.

> **6 to 8 medium-small potatoes**
> **4 tbsp. butter**
> **3 to 4 tbsp. fresh white**
> **breadcrumbs**
> **2 tbsp. parsley, minced**

Scrub the new potatoes but do not peel. Wash and peel old potatoes.

Melt the butter in a heavy metal frying pan, just big enough to hold the potatoes in one layer. Put in the potatoes, cover the pan, and cook over low heat, turning the potatoes several times during the cooking. Cook until they are golden all over. Add the breadcrumbs and shake the pan over medium heat until the breadcrumbs absorb the butter and become crisp. This will take just a few minutes.

If you like coarse salt with your potatoes, replace the breadcrumbs with 1 teaspoon coarse salt and proceed in the same way. Serves 6.

BEST MASHED POTATOES

Through the years, I've tried many ways of preparing mashed potatoes. This is my best recipe – the potatoes are very smooth, white, and creamy. I prefer to pressure-cook them, but they can also be boiled.

> **8 potatoes, peeled and halved**
> **4 tbsp. instant skim milk powder**
> **½ to ¾ cup commercial sour cream**
> **¼ tsp. savory**
> **1 green onion, minced (optional)**
> **salt and pepper, to taste**

Boil the potatoes until tender, then drain and put pan back over heat until the potatoes are dry. Put them through a potato ricer over the cooking pan, add the remainder of the ingredients, and beat until light and smooth.

Variations:

To serve with roast pork or sausages, add 2 cups of cooked mashed turnips to the above recipe and replace the savory with sage.

To serve with chicken, fish, or eggs, add 1½ cups cooked, mashed carrots to the above and replace savory with basil.

To serve with lamb, beef, or hamburger, add 1 cup of onion, fried in bacon fat and mixed with the savory.

POTATO PANCAKES

These are delicious with any pot roast or daube. The leftover pancakes can be frozen.

> 6 potatoes, peeled
> ¼ cup breadcrumbs
> 2 eggs, beaten
> 1 onion, grated
> salt and pepper, to taste
> 2 - 3 tbsp. bacon fat or lard

Grate peeled potatoes and keep in iced water to prevent them from turning black. When ready to make pancakes, drain potatoes and squeeze very dry in a towel (I find a terry cloth towel very effective). Combine potatoes with breadcrumbs, beaten eggs, onion, salt, and pepper.

Heat fat in a frying pan and drop potato mixture, a spoonful at a time, into pan as for pancakes. Brown on one side, turn, and cook until brown on other side. Keep warm in oven. Serve with pickled red cabbage. Serves 6-8.

ELEGANT COLCANNON

I call it by this name because I was inspired by the Irish cabbage and potato colcannon to create this combination with carrots. I sometimes substitute turnips for the carrots, and at other times I add grated cheese (about ½ cup). It goes beautifully with roast turkey or chicken.

> 4 to 6 carrots, peeled and cubed
> 3 medium-sized potatoes, pared
> and cubed
> 1 medium-sized onion, sliced
> ⅛ tsp. dried thyme or ½ tsp. dried
> basil
> 3 tbsp. butter
> milk or water (about ⅔ cup)
> 1 egg
> ¼ cup commercial sour cream
> salt and pepper
> ¼ cup chopped parsley

Place in a saucepan the carrots, potatoes, onion, thyme or basil, and 1 tablespoon of the butter. Add enough water or milk to cover one inch of the bottom. Cover and simmer until the vegetables are tender. This will take 10 to 15 minutes.

If you have a blender, pour in the drained vegetables and add just enough of the cooking liquid to make a thick purée; or make a purée by pressing the vegetables through a food mill or sieve.

To the hot purée, add the egg, sour cream, and the remaining butter. Add salt and pepper to taste. Whip over low heat until creamy and fluffy. Serve sprinkled with parsley. Serves 4-6.

NEW POTATOES IN CUCUMBER SAUCE

To make this ahead of time, cook and peel the potatoes, prepare dressing, cover, and keep both at room temperature. Then they can be combined quickly before heating.

> 18 - 24 small new potatoes
> 5 - 6 green onions, finely chopped
> 1 medium cucumber, unpeeled
>   juice of 1 lemon
> 1 tsp. salt
> ½ tsp. paprika
> 4 tbsp. mayonnaise

Cook the whole potatoes in their skins, drain and then dry them for a few seconds over the heat. Let cool slightly and peel, cutting any large ones into thick slices. Mix in onions and set aside.

Grate the cucumber on a fine grater, removing all seeds. Place in the top of a double boiler with remaining ingredients and stir over boiling water until well blended. Add potatoes and gently stir over simmering water until hot. Serves 10.

SPINACH PANCAKES

Make them large to be eaten with a poached egg on top for lunch or, make them small to be served as a vegetable with roast lamb.

> 3 eggs
> 6 tbsp. flour
> 2 - 3 cups of chopped, barely
>   cooked spinach
> 2 cups cottage cheese
> ½ cup grated cheddar cheese
> ½ tsp. salt

Beat the eggs and flour together. Add the remaining ingredients and stir until well mixed. Place in a buttered 9-inch pie plate for a large pancake or, drop by tablespoon on a buttered baking sheet for the small ones. Bake the large pancake for one hour in a 325°F. oven and the small one for 30 minutes in a 350°F. oven.

These pancakes should really be made with fresh spinach. Wash the spinach and place in a saucepan without any water, as there is always a sufficient amount that clings to the spinach to cook it. Cover and place over high heat for about 4 minutes, turning once. Do not drain the spinach as the liquid is needed to make the custard in the pancake. Serves 4.

BAKED MUSTARD TOMATOES

A must on your list if you are a barbecue fan. This is the perfect vegetable to serve with chops, minced patties, or steaks.

> **firm, medium-sized tomatoes**
> **sugar**
> **French or German-style mustard**
> **dry breadcrumbs**
> **basil, to taste**
> **salt and pepper**
> **butter**

Cut unpeeled tomatoes in half. Place in generously buttered shallow pan or casserole, cut-side up. Sprinkle each half with a pinch of sugar, basil, salt, and pepper. Spread top with a bit of mustard and sprinkle with breadcrumbs. Dot with butter and bake at 375° F. for about 15 to 20 minutes. When ready, cover dish with foil and place on edge of barbecue to keep warm.

BAKED CHEESE AND TOMATO PIE

A pie without crust, flavored tomatoes topped with a cheese custard, it is equally good hot or cold. An excellent summer lunch.

> **1 cup fine fresh breadcrumbs**
> **3 tbsp. soft butter or margarine**
> **2 tbsp. grated Swiss cheese**
> **2 large or 4 medium firm ripe**
> ** tomatoes**
> **½ tsp. honey or sugar**
> **1 tsp. salt**
> **½ tsp. basil**
> **¼ tsp. pepper**
> **2 green onions, chopped fine**
> **1 tbsp. butter**
> **2 eggs, lightly beaten**
> **1 cup light cream or milk**
> **½ cup Swiss or Gouda cheese,**
> ** grated**
> **salt and pepper**

Make the crust by stirring together with your fingers, the breadcrumbs, the 2 tablespoons soft butter, and the 2 tablespoons grated Swiss cheese. Pat in the bottom of an 8 or 9-inch pie plate. Bake in a 400° F. oven for 10 minutes or until lightly browned. Cool on cake rack.

When crust has cooled, slice unpeeled or peeled tomatoes, place in layers on the crust, sprinkle with sugar or honey, salt, basil, pepper, and green onions. Dot with butter.

Beat together the eggs, cream or milk, and grated Swiss or Gouda cheese. Season with salt and pepper to taste. Pour over the tomatoes. Bake in a 375° F. oven for 30 to 40 minutes or until custard has set. Serves 6.

TOMATOES PROVENÇALE

Simple, pungent, colorful, and unforgettable.

4 large (2 lbs.) tomatoes
3 tbsp. olive or salad oil
½ tsp. each, salt and pepper
1 tbsp. sugar
1 clove garlic, crushed
1 tbsp. chopped parsley
1 tsp. basil
2 tbsp. coarse breadcrumbs

Halve tomatoes crosswise and remove seeds by pressing each half in your hand.

Heat the oil in a large frying pan. Place tomatoes in oil, cut side down and cook over medium heat for about 3 minutes. Turn, sprinkle cut side with salt, pepper, and sugar mixed together. Place garlic in the bottom of pan and cook for another two minutes or until the tomatoes are tender.

Remove tomatoes to a heated service platter and sprinkle the tops with parsley and basil mixed together.

Add breadcrumbs to frying pan and stir constantly over high heat until golden brown. Sprinkle over tomatoes and serve. Serves 8.

CHEDDAR BAKED MACARONI

The personality of this baked macaroni is in the combination of grated and diced cheddar. Use strong old cheddar. The tossed breadcrumbs on top can be covered with an addition ½ cup of diced cheddar or Swiss cheese.

16 oz. elbow macaroni
1 cup grated cheddar cheese
1 cup diced cheddar cheese
3 tbsp. butter
½ cup celery, finely chopped
1 onion, minced
4 tbsp. flour
2 cups milk
1 cup light cream
salt and pepper, to taste
½ cup dry breadcrumbs
1 tbsp. melted butter

Cook macaroni according to directions on package. Drain and place half the macaroni in a buttered baking dish. Sprinkle with half of the grated and half the diced cheese. Add the rest of the macaroni and cover with the rest of the cheese.

Melt the butter, add the celery and onion, and simmer for 10 minutes over low heat. Add the flour, mix, then add the milk and cream. Cook until creamy. Salt and pepper to taste. Pour over the macaroni. Toss the breadcrumbs with the melted butter and sprinkle over the macaroni. Bake 40 minutes, uncovered, in a 350° oven. Serves 6.

MY NOODLE CASSEROLE

When I cannot think of what to cook for a light meal, I often prepare this simple casserole. We never tire of it.

8 oz. noodles
1¼ cups plain yogurt or sour cream
8 oz. cottage cheese
¼ cup butter or margarine
½ tsp. salt
¼ tsp. pepper
4 tbsp. chopped parsley
3 green onions, chopped (optional)
1 egg, lightly beaten

Cook noodles according to package directions, then drain. Put back into pan with remaining ingredients and stir with a fork over low heat until heated through. Pour into a 1½-quart casserole (you can prepare this ahead of time) and bake uncovered in a 300° oven for 45 minutes. Serves 6.

GOLDEN RICE SPINACH CASSEROLE

My favorite vegetable casserole with hot baked ham. Also very nice topped with 4 to 6 sliced hard-boiled eggs, served as a main course.

⅓ cup salad oil
1 tbsp. turmeric
¼ tsp. aniseed (optional)
1 onion, chopped fine
1 cup uncooked, short-grain rice
2 cups boiling water
1¼ tsp. salt
1 bag fresh spinach
6 green onions, chopped fine
¼ cup fresh dill or parsley, chopped

Heat the salad oil, add the turmeric and aniseed. Stir quickly over high heat until they are quite hot. Add the onion and the rice, stir a few minutes or until well blended; lower the heat and cook for 10 minutes, stirring often.

Add the boiling water and salt. Bring to a fast boil. Cover and simmer for 15 minutes.

Wash and chop the spinach rather coarsely. Slice the green onions, mix the spinach, onion, dill or parsley.

Make alternate rows of cooked rice and raw mixed greens in a buttered casserole. Salt and pepper each row lightly. Top with a few dots of butter. Cover and bake 30 minutes in a 350° oven. Serves 6.

BAKED BROWN OR WILD RICE

Both are good. The difference is in the cost!

1¼ cups brown or wild rice or
half and half of each
1½ tsp. salt
3 cups boiling water
1 tbsp. butter
1 onion stuck with 4 cloves
1 tbsp. grated fresh ginger root
(optional)

Wash the rice thoroughly under running cold water. Place all the ingredients in a non-metal casserole with a tight-fitting lid, or put foil between cover and casserole. Bury the onion in the middle of the rice. Cover and bake in a preheated 325° F. oven one hour for brown rice, 1½ hours for wild rice. Follow the same procedure if using a mixture of both kinds of rice and bake until tender. Serves 6 to 8.

WILD RICE À LA FERGUSON

Nowadays, 1 cup or ½ cup wild rice should make a main course for 6, because of its cost.

1 cup wild rice
3 tbsp. butter
1 small onion, minced
2 stalks celery, diced
½ cup fresh parsley, minced
¼ tsp. thyme
3 medium carrots, grated
½ lb. strong cheddar cheese, grated
1½ cups chicken stock
2 tbsp. butter, diced

Wash the rice under running water and spread on a towel to dry for 2 hours.

Melt the 3 tablespoons butter in a heavy frying pan. Brown the onions until tender. Remove from frying pan and add the dry wild rice to the remaining butter. Cook, stirring constantly, until a hazelnut fragrance emanates from the rice.

Mix together the celery, parsley, thyme, carrots, and browned onions. Butter a baking dish and fill with alternate layers of wild rice, vegetables and grated cheese, until all the ingredients have been used. Cover with the chicken stock. Dot with butter.

Cover and bake in a 350° oven for one hour.

EASY BARLEY PILAFF

Reheats beautifully even after 3 to 4 days of refrigeration.

4 tbsp. bacon or melted beef fat or
butter
1 lb. pot or pearl barley
1 envelope onion soup mix
1 tsp. salt
1 (4-oz.) can mushrooms,
undrained
5 cups hot water

Melt the fat in a saucepan or an enamel cast-iron casserole. Add the barley and stir constantly over medium heat, until the grains become golden. Add the remaining ingredients. Stir. Cover. Bake for one hour in a 325° F. to 350° F. oven. Serves 8.

CHAPTER 7

SALADS AND SALAD DRESSINGS

STUFFED BEET SALAD

Delicious when served with cold ham or hot roast pork.

6 medium-sized beets
juice of 1 lemon
½ cup celery, chopped fine
1 cup well drained green peas
¼ cup mayonnaise
1 green onion, minced
lettuce

Boil the beets until tender. Peel and chill. Hollow out the center and rub the inside and outside of each beet with a little lemon juice.

Mix the celery, green peas, mayonnaise, green onion, and the rest of the lemon juice. Season to taste. Fill the hollowed beets with the mixture. Set each beet on lettuce leaves. Serves 4.

RAW CARROT SALAD

A very healthy dish that can be made for one as well as for ten, and just as easily. This is an economical, tasty salad to serve with devilled eggs or cold cuts.

long fresh carrots
clear honey
lime or lemon juice
fresh mint, chopped,
or crushed dried mint
or chopped toasted almonds,
or chopped walnuts

Scrub the carrots with a stiff brush. Shred the unpeeled carrots on the fine shredder to make long, thin shreds. Place in a heap in a plate or a dish. Dribble some honey to taste on top. When it has seeped through the carrots, pour some lime or lemon juice over all, also according to taste. Cover with the fresh or dried mint. No salt or pepper is used on it, but if anyone wishes, it should be added at the table, just before eating.

If made ahead of time, keep refrigerated. It improves on standing.

SOUR CREAM, CELERY, AND CABBAGE SALAD

An interesting change from the usual coleslaw, this recipe dates from French colonial days in Quebec.

4 to 6 cups finely shredded cabbage
1 to 1½ cups diced celery
¼ cup fresh parsley, chopped fine
4 green onions, chopped fine
½ cup commercial sour cream
1 tsp. dill seeds or
2 tsp. fresh dill, chopped fine
1 tsp. salt
¼ tsp. pepper
juice ½ a lemon

Toss all the ingredients together gently in a large wooden bowl. Keep refrigerated until ready to serve. Serves 8.

ORANGE AND PIMIENTO SALAD

A wonderfully colorful salad, it teams a fruit and vegetable in a very unusual combination.

6 large oranges
6 sweet red peppers
5 tbsp. salad oil
3 tbsp. wine vinegar
1 tsp. Dijon mustard
salt, to taste

Place oranges in a large bowl of boiling water, leave for 15 minutes, then drain. Peel them when cool enough, removing all cellulose (the white inner skin) and slice thinly.

Remove cores, seeds and membranes from washed peppers and cut into julienne strips. Thoroughly beat remaining ingredients.

Place alternate layers of oranges and peppers in a bowl, sprinkling each layer with the dressing. Chill, and just before serving, stir gently. Serves 6.

SUMMER POTATO SALAD

When you can make this salad with marble-sized new potatoes and garden fresh cucumbers flavored with green basil, it becomes a gourmet's delight.

4 cups sliced boiled potatoes
1 cup cucumber, sliced paper-thin
½ tsp. salt
¼ tsp. freshly ground pepper
3 tbsp. peanut oil
2 tbsp. cider or wine vinegar
½ cup mayonnaise
3 tbsp. rich cream
3 green onions, chopped fine or ¼
cup minced fresh chives
1 tbsp. minced fresh basil or ½ tsp.
dried basil
1 tsp. lemon juice

Be careful not to overcook the potatoes. When using new potatoes, cook with the peel on. Mix in a bowl the potatoes, cucumber, salt, pepper, salad oil, and vinegar. Toss gently. Refrigerate, covered, for 2 hours. Then drain over a colander for 30 minutes.

Mix together the remaining ingredients. Toss into the potato mixture. Taste for seasoning. Serves 6.

GRANDMÈRE'S COOKED DRESSING

Covered and refrigerated, this will keep 4-8 weeks in a glass jar. It is excellent with all types of vegetable salads.

3 tbsp. butter
2 tbsp. all-purpose flour
1½ tsp. salt
1 tsp. dry mustard
1 tbsp. sugar
sprinkling of mace or nutmeg
1¼ cups milk or cream
2 egg yolks
⅓ cup cider vinegar
½ onion, peeled and sliced

Melt the butter in a heavy metal saucepan. Mix in the flour, salt, mustard, sugar, and mace or nutmeg. Blend completely into the butter and add 1 cup of the milk. Cook over low heat, stirring most of the time until mixture is slightly thickened and creamy.

Beat the remaining ¼ cup of milk together with the egg yolks. Stir into the hot mixture, beating well. When well mixed, add the remaining ingredients (be sure to use cider vinegar only). Simmer over low heat until thickened. Cool, remove the onion slices, and refrigerate. Makes 1½ cups.

POTATO "CIVETTE"

A fantastic sort of potato salad, created by a French epicure friend of mine who says it refreshes the palate and enhances the fineness of the meat. I can vouch for the truth of this. Serve it in a black ebony bowl or in gleaming cut glass as the French do.

    16 to 20 small potatoes
    ¼ cup chives or green onion tops,
        chopped fine
    1 tsp. sugar
    ¼ tsp. freshly ground pepper
    ½ tsp. salt
    2 tbsp. olive oil
        juice of 2 lemons

Make sure the potatoes are the same size.

Peel a little band, about an inch wide, around the middle of each scrubbed potato.

Place the potatoes in a steamer (a sort of double boiler with the bottom of its top piece perforated) or in a sieve or colander that can rest on the rim of a pot of boiling water, but well above the water, as the potatoes are steamed, not boiled. Cover pan with cover or foil.

Steam for 20 to 30 minutes or until potatoes are tender. Turn onto a folded cloth and let them cool, until they can be handled. Then remove peel, which almost comes off by itself.

Prepare the dressing while the potatoes cool. Place in a mortar or in a bowl the chives or green onions, sugar, pepper, and salt. Crush this to a paste with the pestle or a wooden spoon, slowly adding the oil and lemon juice alternately. Then stir about 5 minutes until mixture turns sort of creamy. Pour over the potatoes and stir until well mixed. They will take on a lime green color. Set in serving dish. Sprinkle lightly with paprika. Cover with wax paper and keep at room temperature until ready to serve. Serves eight.

TOMATO CUCUMBER SALAD

My family's favorite whenever we have an outdoor barbecue.

    4 tomatoes, sliced
    ¼ cup salad oil
    ¼ cup cider or red wine vinegar
    1 tbsp. parsley, chopped
        dill, fresh or dried, to taste
    3 green onions, finely chopped
        small head of lettuce
    2 cucumbers, peeled and sliced
        salt and papper, to taste

Place the tomatoes in a bowl with the oil, vinegar, parsley, dill, and onions. Refrigerate for one to 2 hours. When ready to serve, shred the lettuce as you would a cabbage, add to tomatoes with the cucumbers, salt, and pepper. Toss lightly until well blended. Serves 4.

LEMON DRESSING

This is an excellent basic dressing for a green salad. A teaspoon of chopped fresh herbs, when available, can make interesting variations; basil, tarragon, chives, parsley, coriander, marjoram or thyme are the best. They must be fresh as must be the lemon juice.

⅔ **cup salad oil**
½ **cup fresh lemon juice**
¼ **tsp. each, sugar and dry mustard**
¼ **tsp. freshly ground black pepper**
1 **whole garlic clove**
1 **tsp. salt**

Place all the ingredients in a screw-top jar and shake vigorously until blended. Remove garlic after a few days; the dressing will keep about a month in a cool place (preferably not the refrigerator). Yield: 1 cup.

CREAMY PINK DRESSING

A large-quantity recipe, because it will keep for months in a cool place. Perfect with all greens, vegetables, and seafood.

1½ **cups sugar**
5 **tsp. salt**
4 **tsp. paprika**
4 **tsp celery seeds**
2 **tsp. dill seeds (optional)**
1½ **cups white or cider vinegar**
1⅓ **cups ketchup**
1 **onion, chopped fine**
2 **cups peanut oil**

Mix together in a bowl, the sugar, salt, paprika, celery, and dill seeds.

Add the remaining ingredients one by one, beating well with a hand beater after each addition. When well blended, place in jam jars. Keep in a cool place or refrigerate. Shake well before using. Yield: 8 cups.

CHAPTER 8

BREADS

Yeast Breads

The cook who bakes good bread – firm, flavorful, fragrant – knows how to knead. When the dough, forming a sort of ball in shape, has been turned out of the bowl onto a lightly floured board, it should be folded over toward you, then pressed down and away from you with the heel of the hand. Turn the ball a quarter circle each time the above-described motion is repeated. One of the secrets of good bread is long patient kneading – 10 15, 20 minutes, the longer the better. Do it as long as your patience allows.

Then let dough rise in a warm place, covered. When doubled in bulk and if an impression remains when pressed with a finger, punch it down and shape. Place in the pan and make sure that the dough never more than doubles in bulk in the pan.

CRUSTY WATER BREAD
This bread toasts beautifully.

1 cup warm water
2 tsp. sugar
2 packages active dry yeast
3 cups warm water or warm potato
water
2 tbsp. lard or shortening
12 cups all-purpose flour
1½ tbsp. salt
5 tbsp. powdered skim milk

Dissolve the sugar in the 1 cup warm water. Add the active dry yeast. Let stand 10 minutes. Stir well.

Add the lard or shortening to the warm water or potato water. Add the well stirred yeast. Mix together.

Add 6 cups of the flour, cup by cup, stirring well after each addition. Add the salt, powdered milk and gradually, the rest of the flour. Knead until smooth and elastic.

Place in a bowl, oil, cover, let rise until double in bulk.

Punch down, divide into 4 equal parts. Shape in round balls. Cover, let rest 10 minutes.

Grease 4 9 x 5-inch loaf pans. Shape bread. Place in pans. Cover and let rise until double in bulk.

Bake in a 400° F. oven for 15 minutes. Reduce heat to 375° F. and bake for 45 minutes more. Yield: 4 loaves.

APPLE CHEESE BREAD

Apple and sharp cheddar combine to give a tangy and sweet flavor to this quick bread. I always keep some frozen for emergencies. Thirty minutes in a 325° oven will thaw it, ready to be served for tea or breakfast, with butter and marmalade.

½ cup shortening
⅔ cup sugar
2 eggs, beaten
1½ cups grated unpeeled apples
½ cup grated sharp cheddar cheese
¼ cup chopped walnuts
2 cups all-purpose flour
1½ tsp. baking powder
½ tsp. each soda and salt

Cream shortening and sugar, add eggs, and mix well. Add apples and nuts, blend everything together. Add sifted dry ingredients and mix lightly. Bake in a well-greased 9 x 5-inch loaf pan in a 350° F. oven for 50 to 60 minutes.

APRICOT BREAD

There are very few top-quality dried apricot quick breads. As they are on the costly side, I like to make sure that the results are always perfect. This method not only makes an excellent bread, it also has a true apricot flavor and color.

½ cup dried apricots
1 large orange
boiling water
½ cup muscat-type raisins
2 tbsp. soft butter
1 cup fine granulated sugar
1 tsp. almond extract
1 egg
½ cup chopped almonds or walnuts
2 cups all-purpose flour
2 tsp. baking powder
½ tsp. baking soda
¼ tsp. salt

Pour enough hot water over the apricots so they will be completely covered. Soak for 30 minutes. Grate the rind of the orange into long slivers, set aside. Squeeze the juice, place in a measuring cup, and add enough boiling water to make 1 cup.

Drain the apricots and pass them through a food chopper with the raisins and orange rind.

Cream the butter and sugar, add the almond extract and the egg, and beat until light and creamy. Add the fruits and chopped nuts. Mix well.

Sift together the flour, baking powder, soda, and salt. Add to the creamed mixture alternately with the orange juice mixture. Pour into a greased and floured 9 x 5 x 3-inch loaf pan. Bake at 350°F. for 50 to 60 minutes. Yield: 1 loaf.

CHOPPED AND GROUND NUT BREAD

Superb made with pecans, very good with walnuts. It is unlike any nut bread I have ever made. I always make two, one to eat and one for the freezer.

> 6 cups all-purpose flour
> 6 tsp. baking powder
> 1 tsp. salt
> 2 cups sugar
> 1 cup coarsely chopped pecans or
> walnuts
> 1 cup ground pecans or walnuts
> 2 eggs, beaten
> 2 cups milk, at room temperature
> 1 tbsp. melted butter
> grated rind of ½ a lemon

Sift together the flour, baking powder, salt, and sugar. Mix in the chopped and ground nuts.

Combine beaten eggs, milk, melted butter, and lemon rind. Pour all at once over the dry ingredients, stirring quickly until well blended.

Turn into two well-greased 8 x 5 x 3-inch loaf pans. Bake at 350°F. for 50 to 60 minutes. Yield: 2 loaves.

BUTTERSCOTCH BREAD

The cherries and nuts almost make a quick fruit loaf of this bread. It is blended, like muffins, with a minimum of mixing.

> 2 cups all-purpose flour
> ½ tsp. salt
> ½ tsp. soda
> 1½ tsp. baking powder
> ½ tsp. nutmeg or allspice
> 1 cup brown sugar
> ¼ cup chopped candied cherries
> ¼ cup chopped walnuts
> 1 cup buttermilk or sour milk
> 1 egg
> 2 tbsp. melted butter

Sift together the flour, salt, soda, allspice or nutmeg, and baking powder. Add the brown sugar and mix thoroughly. Add the cherries and walnuts.

Stir together the buttermilk, egg, and melted butter. Pour all at once over the dry ingredients. Stir quickly, just enough to blend. Pour into a well greased and floured 9 x 5 x 3-inch loaf pan. Let stand for 20 minutes. Bake at 350°F. for one hour. Yield: 1 loaf.

131

THE FLUFFIEST OF PANCAKES

The most perfect and easiest to make of all pancakes. Try them.

2 tbsp. butter or margarine
1 cup all-purpose flour
1 tsp. salt
1 tsp. soda
1 egg
1 to 1¼ cups buttermilk

Heat the griddle or frying pan. Melt the butter. Sift the flour with salt and soda. Add unbeaten egg, then add buttermilk and melted butter. Stir just enough to moisten the flour; a few lumps here and there do not matter. Let stand 3 to 5 minutes; then the batter will look thick and spongy.

Brush the hot pan with salt or melted butter. Fry the pancakes. Yield: 16 to 18 3½-inch pancakes.

BLUEBERRY PANCAKES

A light fluffy pancake with an interesting flavor. Any small berries can replace the blueberries. When using frozen berries, thaw out and drain thoroughly. The juice, slightly thickened, can be used as a sauce.

1 cup all-purpose flour
3 tbsp. baking powder
¼ tsp. salt
1 tbsp. sugar
1 egg
1 cup milk
¼ cup commercial sour cream
2 tbsp. melted butter
½ cup blueberries

Sift together the flour, baking powder, and salt.

Beat together the egg, milk, and sour cream.

Pour milk mixture over dry ingredients and blend with rotary beater until batter is just smooth. Stir in the butter and fold in the blueberries.

Use 2 tablespoons of batter for each pancake. Fry as usual. Serve hot. Yield: 12 pancakes.

A BASIC MUFFIN

Learn this recipe by heart, then think up your own variations so that on the spur of the moment you can produce delicious muffins.

2 cups all-purpose flour
3 tsp. baking powder
2 tbsp. sugar
½ tsp. salt
1 egg, lightly beaten
1 cup milk
3 tbsp. melted butter or other fat

Sift together the flour, baking powder, sugar, and salt. Blend together the beaten egg and milk, Pour all at once over the dry mixture. Stir, do not beat, only until flour is barely moistened. Then add the melted butter and stir barely enough to blend. A muffin batter is at its best when lumpy. Fill a well greased muffin pan ⅔ full. Bake at 400° F. 20 to 25 minutes. Serve piping hot from the oven. Yield: 12 muffins.

Blueberry Muffins: Increase sugar to ¼ cup, add ¼ teaspoon nutmeg or minced fresh marjoram and fold in 1 cup fresh blueberries.

Bran Muffins: Substitute 1 cup bran cereal for 1 cup flour. Replace white sugar for brown. Add ½ cup currants or raisins and 1 tablespoon wheat germ.

Buttermilk Muffins: Replace sweet milk with an equal amount of buttermilk, reduce baking powder to 2½ teaspoons, add ¼ teaspoon soda.

Bacon Muffins: Use bacon fat and fold in 3 slices crisp bacon, crumbled.

BRAN MUFFINS

The smell of bran muffins, somewhat like fresh country air after haying, is so good that it is an incentive to rise early and bake some for breakfast.

2 cups natural bran
½ cup brown sugar
1 tsp. soda
1½ cups all-purpose flour
2 cups buttermilk

Place the bran and brown sugar in a bowl, mix well. Sift together the soda and all-purpose flour. Add to bran and mix. Add buttermilk all at once. Stir just enough to blend. Pour into a well greased muffin pan. Bake at 350° F. for 25 to 30 minutes. Serve hot with honey or apple jelly. Yield: 20 small muffins.

RICH BLUEBERRY MUFFINS

In the winter I replace the fresh blueberries with one cup of well drained crushed pineapple. I often serve both blueberry and pineapple muffins as a hot individual pudding topped with a tangy lemon sauce.

¼ cup butter
3 tbsp. margarine
⅔ cup sugar
1 egg, beaten
2¼ cups all-purpose flour
1 tsp. salt
4 tsp. baking powder
1 - 1¼ cups blueberries
1 cup milk

Cream together the butter, margarine, and sugar. When very light and creamy, add the eggs, beat again until very light. Sift together the flour, salt, and baking powder. Add all at once to the creamy mixture with the milk. Mix just enough to blend and fold in the blueberries. Pour into a well buttered muffin pan. Top each muffin with a few blueberries. Bake in a 400° F. oven, 25 to 30 minutes. Serve hot. Yield: 12 medium muffins.

SPICE MUFFINS

Children or grownups will enjoy finding these in their lunch box. They are equally good hot or cold, with or without butter.

½ cup shortening
½ cup sugar
1 egg
1 cup molasses
3 cups all-purpose flour
1½ tsp. soda
½ tsp. salt
1 tsp. cinnamon
1 tsp. ginger
¼ - ½ tsp. cloves
1 cup hot water

Cream together the shortening, sugar, and egg. When light, add molasses.

Sift together the flour, soda, salt, cinnamon, ginger, and cloves. Add all at once to the molasses mixture. Mix just enough to blend. Then gradually add the hot water. Mix well and pour into well greased muffin pans. Bake in a 375° F. oven for 20 to 25 minutes. Yield: 24 muffins.

CHAPTER 9

DESSERTS

Fruit Desserts

CROQUANTS AUX POMMES

An old recipe from Quebec. Almost like a bonbon. Serve as is, or with ice cream.

Peel, core, and slice 2 large apples. Place in a bowl with ½ cup chopped nuts. Beat 1 egg with 1 cup sugar until well beaten to partly dissolve the sugar. Add 2 tbsp. flour and 1 tsp. baking powder, and ⅛ tsp. salt. Pour into a 9-inch pie plate. Bake 35 minutes in a 375°F. oven, or until top is browned. Chill 6 to 8 hours before serving. Serves 4.

FRESH APRICOT DRESSING FOR FRUIT SALAD

I like this so much that every season I freeze some mashed fresh apricots with sugar and lime juice. In the winter, I thaw the mixture and add the rest of the ingredients to make the dressing.

> **6 - 8 very ripe apricots (about 1**
> **cup mashed)**
> **juice of 1 fresh lime**
> **3 tbsp. sugar**
> **2 tbsp. mayonnaise**
> **1 cup heavy cream, whipped**
> **few drops of yellow food color**

Halve the apricots and remove pits. Blend in a blender for 3 seconds, or force through a sieve to make a purée. Add the lime juice and sugar; stir until well blended. (If you want to freeze the mixture, do it at this point.)

Add the mayonnaise and fold this mixture into the whipped cream. Color to taste.

Pile on fruit salad. For a sophisticated garnish, top with a few green pistachio nuts. Yield: 2½ cups.

FRUIT COMPOTES

Strawberry Compote

Wash and hull 1 quart of strawberries. Place in a bowl and dribble ¼-½ cup of honey over them. Add the grated peel and juice of ½ an orange. Stir gently with your fingertips, cover, and refrigerate.

Raspberry Chantilly Compote

Thaw a 10-oz. pkg. of frozen raspberries, then mash with a fork or in a blender. Put through a sieve to remove seeds. Clean 1 quart of fresh raspberries. Whip 1½ cups of whipping cream, flavor with 2 tbsp. of icing sugar, and 3 tbsp. of brandy or 2 tsp. of vanilla.

Pile the cream in the center of a glass dish, surround with fresh raspberries and gently spread raspberry purée over berries. Serve with a basket of hot biscuits, each guest pouring the compote over the biscuits.

Black Cherry Burgundy Compote

Stem and pit 1 lb. of large B.C. Bing cherries. Place in a pan with ¼ cup of honey and ¼ cup of red Burgundy or port. Cook over low heat until red juice oozes out of the cherries. Stir in 2 tbsp. of cornstarch, and the juice of ½ an orange of 3 tbsp. of rum. Keep stirring until mixture is creamy and transparent and serve hot or cold with hot biscuits.

Superb Peach Berry Compote

Peel and slice enough fresh peaches to fill an 8-oz. measuring cup. Pour them into a serving dish and do the same with an equal quantity of hulled fresh strawberries or blueberries. Mash contents of two 1-pint baskets of raspberries with 3 tbsp. of icing sugar and pour over fruit in bowl. Sprinkle generously with icing sugar, cover, and refrigerate. The mixture is stirred only when you're ready to pour it over the biscuits. Yield: 3-4 cups.

Blueberry or Currant Compote

Stem, wash and dry 4 cups of blueberries or currants and place in a serving dish. Combine ¼ cup of corn syrup, 1 tbsp. of grated orange peel, ¼ cup of fresh orange juice and bring to a boil. Simmer over low heat for 3 minutes, then stir in 3 tbsp. of honey and pour over fruit. Cover and let stand at room temperature and, when cool, refrigerate. If you wish, add 3 tbsp. of orange liqueur or brandy before serving. Yield: 3-4 cups.

FRUIT JUICE SOUFFLÉ

Another creamless soufflé, which makes it low in calories. Vary the fruit juices and each one will be different. If made with grape juice, the color will be gorgeous.

> 2 tsp. unflavored gelatine
> ¼ cup unsweetened grape juice or
> other juice of your choice
> 2 cups hot unsweetened grape juice
> or other juice of your choice
> ¼ cup sugar
> 1 tbsp. fresh lemon juice
> 4 egg whites
> pinch of salt

Soak the gelatine for 5 minutes in the cold grape juice. Pour into hot grape juice with the sugar and lemon juice. Stir until the sugar melts.

Refrigerate until partly set. Then beat with a rotary beater until thick and foamy.

Beat the egg whites with the salt until stiff. Fold them into the grape juice mixture.

Pour into a 1-quart soufflé dish with a 2-inch wax paper collar. Refrigerate from 4 to 12 hours. Serves 6.

COLD LEMON SOUFFLÉ

I sometimes turn this one into a frozen soufflé by placing it overnight in my freezer. Then I serve it with thawed frozen strawberries or raspberries.

> 1 tbsp. unflavored gelatine
> ¼ cup cold water
> 3 egg yolks
> 1 cup sugar
> ⅓ cup fresh lemon juice
>   grated rind of 1 lemon
> 2 cups heavy cream
> 3 egg whites

Soak the gelatine in the cold water for 10 minutes. Then place the container in hot water and simmer until the gelatine is clear.

Beat the egg yolks until pale and lemon colored. Then gradually add sugar and beat until very light and creamy.

Add the lemon juice and rind. Mix well. Pour in the melted gelatine gradually, while beating. Refrigerate until the mixture has the texture of egg whites.

Then whip the cream, beat the egg whites until stiff, and fold into the lemon mixture. Pour into individual molds or a ¾-quart soufflé dish without a collar. Serves 4.

LOW-CALORIE ORANGE SOUFFLÉ

This four-serving soufflé has only 55 calories per serving.

> 4 egg whites
> 2 tbsp. sugar
> 1 tsp. diet liquid sugar
>   grated rind of 1 orange
> 1 tsp. vanilla
> ½ tsp. orange extract

Grease the top of a 1½-quart double boiler with margarine.

Beat the egg whites until stiff but not dry. Add the sugar and the diet liquid sugar, continue beating until some of the sugar has melted. Add the grated orange rind, vanilla, and orange extract. Mix gently until all is well blended.

Pour this mixture gently into the prepared double boiler top. Cover. Then place over hot, not boiling, water. Make sure the bottom of the double boiler top is not touching the water. Cook for 50 minutes. Do not lift the cover.

When ready, remove top of double boiler from water, uncover, and cool.

ORANGE AND LEMON SNOW

Basically snows are sweet, light, fluffy aspics – very nice as garnishes for fruit salads. Vary the fruit juice; frozen undiluted concentrate can be used. It usually comes in 6-oz. cans, so water, apple juice or fresh orange juice can replace the balance of the liquid.

> 1 envelope unflavored gelatine
> ½ cup sugar
> ¼ tsp. salt
> 1½ cups fresh orange juice
> ¼ cup fresh lemon juice
> 2 unbeaten egg whites
>   peel of 1 orange and 1 lemon,
>   grated

Mix the gelatine thoroughly with the sugar and salt in a small saucepan. Add ½ cup of the orange juice. Place over low heat, stirring constantly until the gelatine has dissolved.

Remove from heat and stir in the remaining orange juice and the lemon juice. Chill until slightly thicker than unbeaten egg white.

When ready, add the unbeaten egg whites and the grated peel of orange and lemon, and beat with an electric beater until mixture foams and begins to hold its shape. Spoon into glass dessert dish, or into small molds, and chill until firm.

To serve as a dessert, top with thawed frozen berries of your choice, or a custard sauce made with the remaining 2 egg yolks. Serves 8.

PEAR CHARLOTTE

An old-fashioned bread-and-fruit pudding that is still good. Serve it with cold, rich cream.

> 2 cups peeled and thinly sliced
>   pears
>   grated rind and juice of 1 orange
>   pinch of coriander or cloves
> ¼ cup butter, melted
> 3 egg yolks, beaten
> 3 tbsp. honey
> 3 tbsp. brown sugar
> 2½ cups fluffy, fresh coarse
>   breadcrumbs
> 3 egg whites

Place in a mixing bowl the pears, rind and juice of the oranges, the coriander or cloves, melted butter, egg yolks, honey, and brown sugar. Mix thoroughly. Beat the egg whites until stiff, add the breadcrumbs, mixing them in gently. Fold into the pear mixture. Pour into a well buttered 8-inch baking dish.

Bake in a preheated 350° F. oven for 30 to 35 minutes or until well puffed and golden brown. Serves 4 to 6.

STRAWBERRY RHUBARB COMPOTE

I need superlatives to describe this early summer delight. Serve it in a glass dish with a bowl of whipped or sour cream, or ice cream.

½ cup orange juice
¾ cup sugar
2 lbs. rhubarb, in 2-inch pieces
1 pint fresh strawberries or
1 10-oz. pkg. frozen strawberries

Bring the orange juice and sugar to a boil, then stir until sugar has dissolved. Add rhubarb, simmer over low heat for 5 minutes and remove from heat.

Stir in fresh (cleaned and halved) or frozen strawberries (the hot mixture will thaw them), then refrigerate. Serves 4.

COLD STRAWBERRY SOUFFLÉ

Wonderful to serve all year around as it is made with frozen berries. It has a beautiful pale pink color, and is very attractive garnished with a few rose petals and green leaves.

1 envelope gelatine, unflavored
¼ cup cold water
1 10-oz. pkg. frozen strawberries
4 egg yolks
1 cup sugar
½ tsp. salt
1 cup whipping cream
4 egg whites

Soak the gelatine in the ¼ cup cold water for 5 minutes.

Thaw out the strawberries and put through a sieve to make a purée. Mix together the egg yolks, ½ cup of the sugar and salt. Cook in double boiler, stirring almost constantly, until very light and creamy.

Remove from heat, add the gelatine. Cool and add the strawberries.

Beat the egg whites, add the second half cup of sugar, and beat until stiff.

139

Whip the cream, pour over the stiffly beaten egg whites and fold into the strawberry mixture. Pour into a 2-quart mold or soufflé dish. Keep refrigerated until ready to serve. Serves 8.

STRAWBERRIES NEVERS

I have a friend who sends me a jar of superb homemade Seville orange marmalade every year. I keep it to make this dessert. The preparation is simplicity itself, yet the result is luscious.

> 1 qt. fresh strawberries
> 1 cup Seville orange marmalade
> ¼ cup orange-flavored liqueur, or brandy
> ½ cup fresh orange juice
> 1 tsp. grated orange rind
> 1 tsp. lemon juice
> whipped cream (optional)

Wash strawberries before hulling them. Drain thoroughly on an absorbent towel. Hull.

Mix marmalade over low heat with liqueur or brandy and stir until well blended. Add orange juice gradually, while stirring, until you have a medium-thick sauce. Add orange rind and lemon juice.

Put the strawberries in a cut-glass dish and pour the cooled marmalade sauce over them. Refrigerate for at least 2 hours before serving.

Serve with a bowl of whipped cream sweetened with a little marmalade and flavored with orange-flavored liqueur or brandy. It is good without the cream too. Serves 6-8.

Custards, Puddings, and Mousses

CARAMEL CUSTARD

An elegant way to end a meal. Gentle as a summer breeze – a custard with its own clear caramel sauce.

> 2 cups milk or 1 cup rich cream
> 1 cup milk
> 3 slightly beaten egg yolks
> 2 slightly beaten eggs
> ½ cup sugar
> ½ tsp. vanilla or 1 tsp. orange flower water

Melt an extra ½ cup sugar over low heat in a heavy metal frying pan. Do not stir as the sugar melts and becomes syrupy, but shake the pan occasionally. Pour clear brown syrup into a 1-quart (4-cup size) casserole and rotate casserole to coat it all over with the hot syrup. It will harden as it touches the sides and bottom of casserole. If the casserole gets too hot, hold it with a cloth. Set aside to cool.

Scald the milk or the milk and cream just until a few small bubbles appear around the edge of the saucepan. Beat slightly together the egg yolks, the whole eggs, and the sugar. Slowly stir in the hot milk, beating constantly. Pour into caramelized casserole. Set in pan or bowl on oven rack, pour hot water around the casserole until the water comes almost to the top of the custard.

Bake in a 325°F. oven for 1¼ hours or until knife inserted off center comes out clean. Chill 12 to 24 hours. Unmold onto a large platter and serve. Serves 6.

CARAMEL BREAD PUDDING

I consider this my best bread pudding.

¾ cup brown sugar
1 egg, beaten
2 slices heavily buttered bread
1½ cups milk
1 tsp. vanilla

Pack sugar in a buttered casserole, cut bread into small pieces and place buttered side down on sugar. Mix egg, milk, and vanilla and pour over mixture. Put in oven and bake until nicely browned. Serve with or without cream. Serves 4.

QUEBEC "POUDING AU SUCRE"

In the spring, this pudding is made with soft maple sugar; in the winter this is replaced by dark brown sugar. The pudding is the top layer, the bottom is a clear delicious syrup that is poured over the pudding when served.

½ cup butter
4 cups bread cubes
1 tsp. cinnamon
½ cup granulated sugar
grated rind of ½ an orange or
lemon
2 cups scalded milk
2 eggs, beaten
1 cup maple or brown sugar
3 tbsp. apple juice or water

Melt the butter until nutty brown. Place the bread in a bowl, pour the melted butter on top and add the cinnamon, the ½ cup sugar, and the orange or lemon rind. Mix together thoroughly.

Place in the bottom of a thickly buttered pudding dish the brown or maple syrup and the apple juice or water.

Pour the bread mixture on top. Beat the eggs and the hot milk together, and pour over the bread. Do not mix. Place the dish in a pan of hot water. Bake 40 to 45 minutes in a 350°F. oven. Serve hot or warm, plain or with cream or ice cream. Serves 6.

CARAMEL APPLE CRUMBLE

An unusual apple-crisp type of dessert.

4 large apples
1 cup light brown sugar
½ tsp. cinnamon
2 tbsp. rum
1 cup all-purpose flour
½ tsp. salt
1 cup grated, medium cheddar
cheese
½ cup soft butter

Peel, core, and slice the apples thinly into an 8-inch baking dish. Mix ½ cup of the brown sugar with the cinnamon and rum. Sprinkle on the apples and mix lightly.

Combine flour, salt, grated cheese, butter, and remaining ½ cup of brown sugar.

Crumble mixture evenly over the apples. Bake in a 325° oven for 40 to 45 minutes. Serve warm with sour cream or whipped cream. Serves 4.

CARAMELIZED FLOATING ISLAND

A light, creamy, crunchy Victorian delight, this is one of those recipes that varies with each family. One variation is to replace the first ½ cup of sugar with maple sugar or syrup.

4 eggs, separated
1¼ cups sugar
2½ cups milk
vanilla or nutmeg, to taste

Beat the egg yolks with half a cup of the sugar until fluffy. Beat egg whites until soft peaks appear. Add ¼ cup of sugar and beat again until stiff.

Heat milk to a simmer in a large saucepan, then drop in egg white by heaping tablespoonfuls. When well puffed, turn quickly to cook other side. As soon as done, remove with a skimmer to a hot platter. These egg white balls take but a minute to cook.

Add yolks to milk and stir quickly until you have a lovely golden cream (do not allow it to boil). Flavor to taste and pour over egg whites.

Over medium heat, caramelize remaining sugar with 3 tbsp. of water to obtain a light golden syrup. Using a fork, pour caramel in long shreds over egg snow and let cool. Serves 6.

CREAM OF LIQUEUR

A smart, delectable, miniature dessert with a sophisticated topping of slivered toasted almonds. It gleams in small oriental dessert dishes, and should be accompanied by a bottle of the same liqueur chosen to make it, in a liqueur glass for each person, not to sip but to use as a measure to pour over the dessert. It is a lovely ending to a meal.

 1¼ **cups light cream**
 1½ **envelopes of unflavored gelatine**
  3 **egg yolks**
 ½ **cup sugar**
    a pinch of salt
 ⅓ **cup liqueur of your choice***
  3 **egg whites**
 ⅓ **cup slivered almonds**

Measure the cream in a saucepan. Add the gelatine and let stand 5 minutes. Then stir over low heat until gelatine melts. Beat the egg yolks with the sugar and salt. Add to the hot milk, stir together for 5 or 6 minutes. Remove from heat, stir in the liqueur.

Beat the egg whites until stiff and fold into the gelatine mixture. When well mixed, pour into individual dishes. Refrigerate at least 4 hours or overnight.

Place the slivered almonds on a baking sheet and set in a 325° oven until toasted, about 20 minutes. Cool, set aside. When ready to serve sprinkle to taste over each dish of cream. Serves 8.

* *Benedictine, B and B, Cointreau, Kahlua Coffee liqueur, Crème de Menthe, rum, brandy,* or *bourbon* are all equally good. Each one gives the dessert a different flavor.

GOLDEN SNOW FLUFF

Cool and light, this dessert is superb served with fresh strawberries, sweetened with Cointreau, Grand Marnier, or sugar. The sauce is served separately.

> **2 envelopes unflavored gelatine**
> **½ cup boiling water**
> **1 cup sugar**
> **½ tsp. salt**
> **1 cup fresh grapefruit juice**
> **1 cup fresh orange juice**
> **4 eggs, separated**
> **2 cups light cream or milk**
> **⅓ cup sugar**
> **pinch of salt**
> **grated peel of 1 orange**

Soak the gelatine in ½ cup of cold water for 5 minutes. Add boiling water and stir until gelatine has dissolved. Add sugar, salt, and stir again to dissolve sugar (over low heat, if necessary). Add 2 juices, mix, and refrigerate until the consistency is that of unbeaten egg whites. Then beat until fluffy with a rotary beater.

Beat egg whites until stiff and fold into fruit fluff. Pour into a glass dish, cover, and refrigerate until set.

Orange Custard Sauce: Beat egg yolks with cream or milk, sugar, and salt. Cook in top of a double boiler over medium-high heat to a light custard consistency, stirring often. Add orange peel, pour into a jug, and refrigerate. Serves 10.

RED WINE JELLY

A cool colorful dessert to be made a day or so ahead and served as is or surrounded with sweetened berries or topped with strawberry ice cream.

> **2 tbsp. unflavored gelatine**
> **¼ cup cold water**
> **2 slices lemon peel**
> **1 cup boiling water**
> **½ cup sugar**
> **1 cup gooseberry jelly**
> **1 cup dry red wine**
> **2 tbsp. brandy or lemon juice**

Soak the gelatine in the cold water for 5 minutes. In a saucepan, simmer lemon peel, boiling water, sugar, and jelly over low heat until sugar and jelly have dissolved.

Add gelatine, stir to dissolve, then put mixture through a sieve. Add remaining ingredients, pour into individual molds or a 1-quart one, and refrigerate. Serves 6.

CHOCOLATE MOUSSE

This is party fare and will please all who come to sit at your table.

1 6-oz. package chocolate chips
6 egg yolks
2 tsp. vanilla or 1 tbsp. rum
6 egg whites

In a double boiler, over hot, not boiling water, melt chocolate chips. Remove from heat. Beat in the egg yolks and vanilla or rum. Stir until well mixed.

Beat the egg whites until stiff but not dry and fold into the chocolate mixture. Spoon into 8 or 10 small fancy dishes or use demi-tasse cups. Cover each dish. Refrigerate overnight.

To serve, top with whipped cream or chocolate curls. To make, peel off curls from a square of unsweetened chocolate with a vegetable parer or a small paring knife. Serves 8 or 10.

CHOCOLATE SOUFFLÉ

One of the most popular of all cold soufflés. I sometimes replace the ordinary semi-sweet chocolate with imported Swiss chocolate – 150 to 200 grams weight (indicated on label) is needed to replace the 5 ounces of semi-sweet chocolate called for in this recipe. Each type of chocolate gives a different flavor to the soufflé.

2 envelopes unflavored gelatine
¼ cup rum or orange juice
5 (1 ounce each) squares
semi-sweet chocolate
⅔ cup milk
5 egg yolks
⅔ cup sugar
1 tsp. vanilla
1½ cups heavy cream
5 egg whites

Sprinkle the gelatine over the rum or orange juice. Let stand 10 minutes. Melt the chocolate over hot water with the milk. Heat until smooth. Add the gelatine and stir until melted. Pour into a bowl to cool.

Place the egg yolks and the sugar on top of a double boiler (do not bother to wash out the chocolate that remains). Beat together with a whisk or rotary beater until very thick and creamy, about 5 to 6 minutes. Do this over hot, but not boiling water. Remove from the hot water and beat about 3 to 4 minutes to cool it off. Then add the vanilla and the chocolate mixture. Refrigerate until cold and partly set. Whip the cream and the egg whites separately. Beat into the partly set chocolate mixture. Make a wax-paper collar around a ¾-quart straight-sided soufflé or baking dish that is suitable for serving. Pour mixture into dish.

Refrigerate for 4 to 12 hours. Remove collar and sprinkle top and sides with icing sugar. Serves 6.

Pies

OLD-FASHIONED PIE CRUST

This pie crust will keep for 2 to 3 months in the freezer or for 3 weeks in the refrigerator, so always have some on hand.

> **5 cups all-purpose flour**
> **1 tsp. salt**
> **1 tbsp. sugar**
> **¼ tsp. soda**
> **1⅓ cups lard**
> **1 egg**
> **3 tbsp. white vinegar**
> **cold water**

Stir together in a bowl the flour, salt, sugar, and soda. Cut in the lard, in fairly large pieces, with two knives or your hands.

Beat together the egg and vinegar. Add enough cold water to make one cup. Add it all at once to the flour mixture. Stir with your hands until mixture comes away from bowl. Shape it into a ball and wrap with transparent film. Refrigerate overnight. Yield: 6 9-inch pie shells.

ENGLISH APPLE PIE

An apple sherry custard in a crust.

> **unbaked pie crust**
> **6 to 8 large apples**
> **¼ cup butter**
> **¾ cup sugar**
> **3 eggs, slightly beaten**
> **grated rind ½ lemon**
> **2 tbsp. lemon juice**
> **1½ tbsp. sherry**
> **few grains salt**

Line pie plate with pastry. Set in refrigerator until ready to be filled.

Pare, core, steam apples. Rub through a fine sieve. Add remaining ingredients. Pour into pie crust. Set in 450° F. preheated oven for 10 minutes, then lower heat to 325° F. and bake 30 minutes more.

SCOTCH APPLE PIE

A sort of apple crisp in a pie.

1 9-inch pie shell, unbaked
6 - 8 apples
¾ cup brown sugar
¼ cup hot water
1 egg, well beaten
¾ cup graham cracker crumbs
¼ cup pastry flour
1 tsp. cinnamon
¼ tsp. nutmeg
⅛ tsp. ginger
4 tbsp. shortening or butter, softened

Line a 9-inch pie plate with a pastry of your choice. Peel the apples, core, and cut into 8 sections lengthwise and set them attractively into the unbaked pie shell. Mix together the brown sugar and hot water. Add the well beaten egg. Pour this mixture over the apples. Mix together the cracker crumbs, flour, spices, and shortening or the softened butter, and sprinkle over the apples.

Bake in a 450°F. oven until it starts to brown, approximately 20 minutes. Reduce heat to 325°F. and continue baking another 20 minutes. Serve warm with, or without, cheese.

MY MOTHER'S BLUEBERRY PIE

This recipe gives one the sensation of eating fresh uncooked blueberries.

baked pie shell
4 cups blueberries
¼ cup water
⅔ cup sugar
2 tbsp. cornstarch
2 tbsp. cold water
whipped cream

Line a 9-inch pie plate with the pastry of your choice. Bake in a 400°F. oven. Unmold and cool.

Wash and clean the blueberries. Cook three-quarters of a cup of blueberries with water until tender. Force through a sieve or put through a food mill to thoroughly mash them. Place the purée in a saucepan, add the sugar and the cornstarch blended with the cold water. Cook over medium heat, stirring constantly, until smooth, transparent, and creamy. Pour this sauce (very hot) over the remaining blueberries. Mix well. Cover and refrigerate until ready to serve.

To serve, pour the blueberry cream into the cooked pie shell and garnish with whipped cream, sweetened to taste.

BRANDY MINCEMEAT PIE

You can start with commercial mincemeat and no one will ever know.

pastry for 2-crust pie
2 cups mincemeat of your choice
2 apples
¾ cup raisins
½ cup brandy
1 tbsp. butter, diced

Place the mincemeat in a bowl. Grate the unpeeled apples on a medium grater, over the mincemeat and add the raisins and half of the brandy.

Line the pie plate with pastry. Pour in the mincemeat. Dot with the diced butter and pour the rest of the brandy on top. Cover with pastry. Bake in a 375°F. oven for 40 minutes. Serve hot or cold.

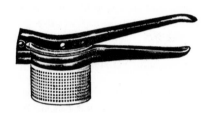

FROZEN LEMON CHIFFON PIE

In the early summer, I usually freeze 6 to 8 of these pies. They make instant desserts that can turn into dramatic ones when topped with fresh strawberries, raspberries, or slices of peaches and flavored with brandy or orange liqueur and sweetened to taste.

3 egg yolks, well beaten
¼ cup fresh lemon juice
2 tsp. lemon peel, grated
pinch of salt
½ cup sugar
3 egg whites, stiffly beaten
1 cup whipping cream
1 tbsp. sugar
¾ cup vanilla or lemon wafers,
crushed

Place in the top of a double boiler the egg yolks, lemon juice, grated lemon peel, salt, and sugar. Place over hot water and stir until well blended. Cook until thick enough to coat a spoon. Stir often. Remove from hot water. Cool until almost cold, then fold in the beaten egg whites. Whip the cream and fold into the lemon mixture.

Sprinkle the bottom of an 8-inch pie plate, lightly buttered, with ½ cup of the crushed vanilla wafers. Pour the mixture into it and sprinkle the rest of the crushed wafers on top. Freeze and serve frozen. This pie is at its best when not allowed to become soft. Serves 6.

MAPLE RAISIN NUT PIE

Raisins and maple syrup always go well together.

unbaked pie crust
1 cup seedless raisins
3 tbsp. flour
1 tbsp. butter
½ cup brown sugar
½ tsp. salt
2 eggs
1½ cups chopped walnuts
1 cup maple syrup
few grains nutmeg

Line pie plate with pastry. Store in the refrigerator until ready to be filled.

Wash, soak, and thoroughly drain raisins. Mix with 1 tablespoon flour in order to separate them well. Spread over bottom of pie crush.

Cream butter. Add brown sugar, salt, well beaten eggs, and the remaining 2 tablespoons flour. Beat until smooth. Stir in walnuts a few at a time. Gradually add maple syrup.

Pour mixture over raisins in pie crust. Set in 450°F. preheated oven and bake for 10 minutes, then lower heat to 325°F. and bake 25 to 30 minutes more.

MAPLE SYRUP PIE

There are many traditional ways of making maple syrup pie. This is how it is made with fresh April syrup when it is so rich and creamy.

1 cup maple syrup
1 cup milk
2 tbsp. butter
2 egg yolks
1 tbsp. water
2 tbsp. cornstarch
⅛ tsp. salt
1 tsp. vanilla
one 9-inch baked pie shell

Place in a saucepan the maple syrup, milk, and butter. Heat over low heat, stirring often, but do not boil.

Beat together the egg yolks and water, then add the remaining ingredients. Mix thoroughly. Add to hot syrup and cook until just thickened, stirring most of the time. Pour while hot into the baked pie shell.

Beat the remaining 2 egg whites until stiff, gradually adding 4 tablespoons sugar, ⅛ teaspoon cream of tartar, and a pinch of salt. Then beat for 5 minutes (a mixer can be used). Spread the meringue on the hot pie filling. Cook to a gentle brown in a preheated 325°F. oven.

Cool pie on a wire cake rack. Serve cold, but not refrigerated. Serves 6.

BUTTER TARTS

A Victorian delight!

unbaked tart shells
3 tbsp. butter
1 cup brown sugar
1 egg
½ tsp. salt
¼ cup seedless raisins
½ cup raisins
½ tsp. vanilla

Cream the butter. Add the brown sugar gradually. Cream until light. Beat the egg and add, little by little to the creamed mixture, stirring after each addition. Stir in the raisins and vanilla. Place one spoonful of this mixture into each tart shell.

Bake for 8 minutes in a preheated oven, the temperature depending on the type of pastry chosen. Lower heat to 375° F. and bake until the filling has set and the crust has browned (10 to 12 minutes more).

Cakes and Frostings

APPLESAUCE CAKE

Use either canned or homemade applesauce for this moist, delicious cake. Wrapped in foil, it will keep 2 weeks in the bread box and 6 weeks in the refrigerator.

3 cups all-purpose flour
¼ tsp. cloves
1 tsp. cinnamon
¼ tsp. nutmeg
½ tsp. allspice or cardamom
3 tbsp. cocoa
2½ tsp. baking soda
1 tsp. salt
1 cup chopped nuts
⅔ cup chopped raisins
1½ cups chopped dates
1 cup brown sugar
¾ cup shortening
3 eggs
2 cups applesauce

Sift together the flour, cloves, cinnamon, nutmeg, allspice or cardamom, cocoa, baking soda, and salt. Add the nuts, raisins, and dates, then stir until the nuts and fruits are well coated.

Combine the brown sugar, shortening, and eggs and beat for 5 minutes with an electric beater. Add the fruit-flour mixture and the applesauce, then stir until well blended.

Pour into 2 greased and floured 9 x 5 inch loaf pans or one 10-inch tube pan. In either case, bake at 350° F. for 1 hour and 20 minutes. Let stand for 10 minutes, then unmold and cool on a cake rack.

ELEGANT AND CASUAL BABA AU RHUM

With this recipe, even a cake mix can fool people into thinking they are eating the real baba, which has a yeast base. Make it the day before – garnish with cream the day of the party – keep refrigerated.

The cream can be replaced by ice cream or both can be omitted and the rum cake served flambé.

> 1 box yellow cake mix of your
>   choice
> ½ cup sugar
> ½ cup water
> ½ cup dark rum
> 1 cup whipping cream
> 3 tbsp. icing sugar
> 2 tbsp. dark rum

Butter an 8-inch ring mold pan very thoroughly, then sprinkle with sugar and shake pan to remove excess. Mix the cake according to package directions. Pour enough of the batter into the prepared mold to reach to a little more than half way up the mold. Bake in a preheated oven 25 to 30 minutes or until a toothpick inserted in the cake comes out with no batter clinging to it. Let stand on cake rack for 10 minutes before unmolding.

While cake is baking, combine the sugar with the water and stir over medium heat until sugar has dissolved. Take off the heat and stir in the rum. Unmold the cake on a service plate and pour the hot syrup over the hot cake. It will soak in immediately. If any syrup remains on the plate, spoon it gradually on the cake. Do not refrigerate, even overnight.

To serve, fill center of ring with the cream, whipped and flavored with the sugar and rum. Garnish cream with rose petals or candied violets.

BANANA WALNUT CAKE

If you just happen to have some sour cream on hand and a couple of overripe bananas, try this superb cake. It will disappear so quickly you will not have to worry about storing it.

> ½ cup shortening
> ½ cup sugar
> 2 beaten eggs
> 4 tbsp. sour cream
> 1 cup all-purpose flour
> 1 tsp. baking soda
> ½ tsp. salt
> 1 cup chopped walnuts (optional)
> 1 cup mashed bananas

Cream together the shortening and sugar. Beat the eggs with the sour cream, then add to the shortening mixture and beat until very light and creamy.

Sift together the flour, baking powder, baking soda, and salt. If you are using the walnuts, stir them into the flour mixture until they are well coated.

Add the mashed bananas to the creamy mixture, mix well, then add the flour mixture. Stir just enough to blend and pour into a well greased 10-inch ring pan, or a 9 x 5-inch bread pan. Bake at 350°F. for 30-35 minutes and cool on a cake rack.

151

ANNETTE'S CHOCOLATE CAKE

Annette has a flair for cake making. This chocolate cake is one of her masterpieces. Do not worry about the quite thin batter, that is as it should be. The result is a dark, full-flavored chocolate cake with a sponge-cake texture.

2 ounces unsweetened chocolate
1 cup milk
2 tbsp. butter
1 cup sugar
1 egg yolk
1 cup all-purpose flour
1 tsp. soda

Melt the chocolate over very low heat in a heavy metal saucepan. Add ½ cup of the milk and stir until thick. Remove from heat. Add the butter and stir until melted. Add the sugar. Mix and stir in the egg yolks. Mix thoroughly. Stir the soda with the flour and add to the chocolate mixture, alternately with the other ½ cup milk. Beat well. Pour into a greased and floured 8 x 8 x 2-inch cake pan. Bake at 375°F. for 30 minutes. Frost as you wish. I like mine just as is. Yield: 9 servings.

CHOCOLATE POUND CAKE

We rarely meet chocolate pound cake, but this one, garnished with finely chopped walnuts, is an especially good one.

1 cup soft margarine
2 cups fine granulated sugar
2½ cups all-purpose flour
1 tsp. salt
1 tsp. baking powder
1 tsp. vanilla
4 eggs
1 cup buttermilk
3 (1 oz.) squares unsweetened
   chocolate
1 tbsp. powdered instant coffee
1 cup nuts, chopped fine

Cream together the margarine and sugar until very light and creamy.

Sift together the flour, salt, and baking powder and add to the creamed mixture. Stir in the vanilla. Add the eggs, one at a time, beating well at each addition. Add the buttermilk and mix thoroughly.

Melt the chocolate over hot water, stir in the instant coffee. Cool slightly. Add to the batter, mix well, and fold in the chopped nuts.

Bake in a slightly greased and floured 9 x 5-inch loaf pan, lined with greased wax paper in a 350°F. oven for about 55 minutes. Unmold and cool on wire cake rack.

Sprinkle with icing sugar or top with Fluffy Chocolate Cream.

FLUFFY CHOCOLATE CREAM

A creamy, light topping for any cake. The semi-sweet chocolate replaces the sugar.

1 tbsp. instant coffee
2 tbsp. hot water
4 ounces semi-sweet chocolate
¼ cup heavy cream

Place the coffee and water in top of a double boiler, stir to dissolve, and add the chocolate. Melt, stirring a few times. Cool the chocolate for 15 minutes. Whip the cream and fold into the cooled chocolate. Fluff on top of cake.

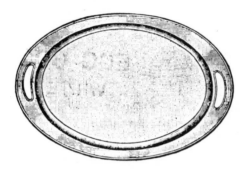

CINNAMON BUTTERMILK CAKE

Sour milk can replace the buttermilk. Nutmeg in equal quantity can replace the cinnamon. Whichever way you make it, this cake is delicious.

½ cup margarine or shortening
1¼ cups light brown sugar
2 eggs
1 cup buttermilk
2 cups all-purpose flour
1 tsp. soda
½ tsp. salt
1 tbsp. cinnamon

Cream margarine or shortening, add brown sugar and eggs gradually. Beat until very light. Alternately add buttermilk and the dry ingredients sifted together, beating well after each addition until batter is smooth.

Grease and line two 8-inch layer cake pans with wax paper. Divide batter equally into each pan. Bake at 350° F. for about 25 to 30 minutes. Fill and frost with a coffee frosting. Yield: 10 to 12 servings.

PINEAPPLE ICEBOX CAKE

If you like to prepare your dessert a day ahead, success will be yours with this one.

1 20-oz. can crushed pineapple
1 cup sugar
  juice of ½ a lemon
  juice of ½ an orange
½ cup water
2 egg yolks
3 tbsp. cornstarch
2 beaten egg whites
10 - 14 lady fingers
  whipped cream, ice cream, or
  grated sweet chocolate

Drain the pineapple well, but reserve the liquid.

In the top of a double boiler, mix the pineapple, sugar, lemon and orange juice, water, and egg yolks. Blend the cornstarch with 3 tablespoons of the reserved pineapple juice. Add this to the mixture and cook over boiling water, stirring often until it is thick and creamy. Cool completely. Fold in the beaten egg whites.

Line the bottom and sides of a 9-inch buttered spring form pan with lady fingers (if they are double, split them in two). Fill the lined mold with the pineapple mixture and refrigerate for at least 12 hours.

When ready to serve, top with sweetened whipped cream, balls of ice cream, grated sweet chocolate, or serve it plain. Serves 4-6.

BUTTER CRUMB GINGERBREAD

This is a delicious, crunchy, butter-topped gingerbread with a golden color. It keeps very well. I found this recipe in a 1935 English magazine, and to this day I have baked it with the same excellent results.

2 cups cake flour or
1⅔ cups all-purpose flour
1 tsp. baking soda
1 cup sugar
1 tsp. cinnamon
2 tsp. ginger
¼ tsp. salt
½ cup shortening or soft chicken fat
2 tbsp. molasses
1 egg
1 cup buttermilk

Topping:
2 tbsp. butter, very soft
1 tbsp. flour
4 tbsp. sugar
½ tsp. cinnamon or ginger

Sift together, three times, the flour, soda, sugar, cinnamon, ginger, and salt. Cut in the shortening or chicken fat until a fine crumb mixture is obtained. Beat the molasses and egg well and add to the crumb mixture. Add the buttermilk. Mix well and pour into a greased 8 x 8 x 2-inch pan.

For the topping, spread the very soft butter lightly over the top. Mix together the flour, sugar, and cinnamon or ginger and sprinkle on top of the buttered batter. Bake at 350° for 45 minutes.

HOT MILK CAKE

The most versatile of cakes – not a true sponge cake as it contains baking powder and hot milk, but nevertheless it has a velvety light texture – good with a light icing or, for a treat, whipped cream and sweetened sliced strawberries.

> 2 eggs
> 1 cup sugar
> 1 cup sifted pastry flour
> ⅛ tsp. salt
> 1 tsp. baking powder
> 1 tbsp. butter
> ½ cup boiling milk

Beat the eggs until light and foamy. Add the sugar and beat for 5 minutes. Add all at once the sifted flour, salt, and baking powder. Mix well.

Melt the butter into the boiling milk and pour it all at once into the batter. Quickly mix and turn into an 8 x 8-inch greased cake pan. Bake in a preheated 350° F. oven 30 minutes. Yield: 10 servings.

MAPLE TOURLOUCHE

This is a sort of quick upside-down cake and a must in the sugaring season in eastern Canada. It should be served hot with cold rich cream poured on top. As a variation, add some chopped walnuts to the hot syrup.

> 1 cup maple syrup
> 1 tbsp. soft butter
> 3 tbsp. sugar
> 1 egg
> 1 cup all-purpose flour
> 2 tsp. baking powder
> ⅛ tsp. salt
> ¼ tsp. nutmeg or cinnamon
> ½ cup milk

Bring syrup to a boil and pour into a generously buttered 8 x 8 x 2-inch baking dish. Let stand in a warm place. With a large spoon or blending fork, beat butter, sugar, and egg together until creamy.

Mix remaining dry ingredients and add with the milk to creamed mixture, stirring until well blended. Place as four large balls into hot syrup, then stretch dough with two forks until all are joined together. This is easy because the dough gets very soft when it comes in contact with the hot syrup.

Bake at 350° for 30 minutes, or until golden brown. When done, invert on a platter or serve directly from pan.

PERFECT ENGLISH TRIFLE

Homemade sponge cake, black currant jam, dry, dry sherry, and a true old-fashioned boiled custard are all brought together to perfection, then refrigerated for 12 hours.

> 1 8-inch sponge cake
> 1 cup black currant jam
> ½ cup dry sherry
> 4 egg yolks
> ¾ cup sugar
> 1½ tbsp. arrowroot or flour
> ¼ tsp. salt
> 1 cup milk
> 2 cups light cream
> 1 tbsp. vanilla (no error)

Place in top of a double boiler the egg yolks, sugar, arrowroot or flour, and salt. Beat together until thoroughly blended. Scald the milk and cream. Add to egg yolk mixture. Then cook over boiling water until custard thickens slightly, stirring constantly. This may take 15 to 20 minutes. Then, as soon as ready, pass custard through a fine strainer. Add vanilla. Cover bowl tightly with transparent paper. Refrigerate until needed.

To make the trifle: Line a cut-glass bowl with fingers of sponge cake. Spread cake with some of the jam and sprinkle with sherry – make these layers until all the cake, jam and sherry have been used up. Pour the custard (hot or cold) over all. Cover bowl and refrigerate for 12 hours. To serve, top with whipped cream and toasted chopped almonds. Serves 6 to 8.

SPONGE CAKE

I have made this cake for years for trifle or to serve with fresh strawberries and cream.

> 3 eggs
> 1½ cups fine granulated sugar
> 2 cups sifted pastry flour
> 1½ tsp. baking powder
> ½ cup cold water
> ½ tsp. salt
> ½ to 1 tsp. almond or vanilla
>   extract

Beat whole eggs for 2 minutes in an electric mixer or with rotary beaters. Add the sugar and beat for 5 minutes. Sift flour and baking powder together 3 times. Add to egg mixture all at once. Beat for 2 minutes. Add the cold water, salt, and extract. Beat for one minute.

Turn the batter into an ungreased 8 x 8-inch pan. Bake in a preheated 425°F. oven for 25 minutes. Invert, cool, and unmold.

DIVINE STRAWBERRY TORTE

A wonderful party dessert. The strawberries may be replaced with raspberries, peaches, or blueberries, depending on the season and everything can be done ahead of time.

> ½ cup egg whites
> 1 tbsp. lemon juice
> pinch of salt
> 1⅓ cups fine granulated sugar
> ½ cup flaked coconut
> 2 egg yolks
> pinch of salt
> 2 tbsp. lemon juice
> 2 tbsp. sugar
> 1 tbsp. cornstarch
> ½ cup water
> 1 cup whipping cream
> 1 - 2 pints fresh strawberries

Using hand mixer or electric beater, beat egg whites with lemon juice and salt until soft peaks have formed. Add sugar, 3 tbsp. at a time, beating hard after each addition. Keep beating until very stiff, 10-15 minutes in all. Gently fold in coconut.

Mark a 9-inch circle on a baking sheet and grease inside lightly. Turn meringue into center of circle and carefully spread to edges, building up until about 2 inches high around outside and slightly lower in center. Enclose outer edge with a 2-inch foil collar.

Place in an oven that has been at 400° for 15 minutes. Immediately turn heat off and let meringue stand in closed oven for 5 hours. Open door and leave in oven 5 hours or overnight.

To make lemon sauce: beat egg yolks with salt, lemon juice, and sugar. Stir in cornstarch and water. Cook in a double boiler or over low heat until mixture thickens, beating often. Refrigerate covered until cold, then fold in cream whipped until stiff.

To serve, slip meringue shell on to a serving plate with a large spatula. Top with the lemon cream and arrange sweetened berries on top. Serve at once or refrigerate for 2 hours.

PLAIN JANE TURNOVER NUT CAKE

The cake itself is a perfect one egg cake, which can be used for all recipes calling for a plain cake. A reader who signed herself "Plain Jane" sent this recipe to me 10 or 12 years ago. I have been using it ever since.

3 tbsp. butter or margarine
½ cup brown sugar
2 tbsp. all-purpose flour
½ cup chopped walnuts
½ cup butter, margarine or
  shortening
1 cup sugar
1 egg
1 tsp. vanilla or other extract
1⅔ cups all-purpose flour
2 tsp. baking powder
¼ tsp. salt
½ cup milk

Cream together the 3 tablespoons butter, brown sugar, and the 2 tablespoons flour. Add the chopped walnuts. Spread in the bottom of an 8 x 8-inch well greased cake pan.

Beat the ½ cup butter, margarine, or shortening until creamy. Add the sugar, egg, and vanilla gradually, and beat together until very fluffy. Sift together the flour, baking powder, and salt.

Beat alternately with the milk into the creamed mixture. Spoon on top of the nut filling. Bake at 350° F. for 35 to 40 minutes. Cool on cake rack for 10 minutes and unmold. Yield: 6 to 8 servings.

TRADITIONAL WHITE FRUIT CAKE

Wrap in a wine or brandy-soaked cloth and foil, store in cool place – this cake will keep for a year. An elegant cake, serve it very thinly sliced.

2 cups almonds, blanched and
  slivered
1½ cups (10 oz.) diced citron peel
1½ cups diced orange peel
½ cup diced lemon peel
1½ cups candied green cherries
1½ cups white raisins
4 cups all-purpose flour
½ tsp. salt
1 tsp. nutmeg
1 tsp. nutmeg
1 lb. soft butter
2 cups sugar
10 eggs
1 tsp. vanilla
1 tsp. grated lemon rind
2 tbsp. brandy (optional)

Grease two 9 x 5 x 3-inch loaf pans or 4 small loaf pans or 4 1-lb. coffee cans. Line with a double thickness of wax paper. Grease paper.

Place in a large bowl, the almonds, citron, orange and lemon peels, candied cherries, and white raisins.

Sift together the flour, salt, and nutmeg. Take out half a cup and add to the fruits, mixing well, to make sure that all the fruits are coated.

In a mixer or with an electric hand beater, cream the butter and gradually add the sugar. When fluffy, add the eggs, one at a time. Then add the vanilla, lemon rind, and brandy.

Add the flour half a cup at a time, beating at low speed after each addition.

Add batter to floured fruits and nuts. Then stir and mix with your hands until everything is thoroughly blended. Place in prepared pans.

Place a shallow pan of water on oven floor. Preheat oven to 300° F. Bake cake for 3 hours for the large, 2 hours for the small or, until a cake tester comes out clean.

Let cool completely on cake rack before unmolding. Unmold and wrap.

KENT YULETIDE CAKE

An old Kentish recipe, a superb, traditional fruit cake. It is made with self-rising flour. The longer this cake is kept, the better it is. I like to make it at least 3 weeks before Christmas.

1 cup unsalted butter
1⅔ cups brown sugar
5 eggs
2 tsp. molasses
1½ cups seedless raisins
¾ cup diced, mixed peel
1 cup muscat raisins
½ cup chopped almonds
2 tbsp. allspice
½ tsp. salt
3 cups self-rising flour
⅓ cup brandy

Cream the butter and brown sugar until light. Add the eggs, one at a time, beating well after each addition. Add the molasses and beat.

In a large bowl, mix the seedless raisins, mixed peel, candied cherries, currants, muscat raisins, almonds, allspice, salt, and self-rising flour. Stir with your hands until well blended together.

Add to the egg mixture and again stir with your hands until very well blended. Add the brandy and mix thoroughly.

Butter a 10-inch cake pan, 4 inches deep, then line the bottom with wax paper. Pour in the batter.

Bake 3 to 3½ hours in a 300° F. oven in the middle shelf.

Cool completely in the pan (set on a rack before unmolding). Remove the wax paper.

To keep, wrap the cake in a cheesecloth dipped in brandy and then in clear plastic wrap and foil. Refrigerate or keep in a cool place.

It will keep for 12 to 16 months, refrigerated. It can be cut in four to make wedges of Christmas cake to be covered with thinly rolled almond paste. Serves 10 to 15.

BUTTER FROSTING AND VARIATIONS

It is hard to go wrong with this basic frosting.

¼ cup butter
2 cups icing sugar
⅛ tsp. salt
3 tbsp. water, juice, milk, or cream
1 tsp. vanilla

Cream the butter and add 1 cup of the icing sugar gradually, while stirring. When very creamy, add the second cup of icing sugar and the salt alternating with the liquid of your choice. Add the vanilla and beat, adding a bit of sugar or liquid, if necessary, to get just the proper consistency.

Chocolate Frosting: Add ⅓ cup cocoa, sifted with the sugar, or 2 ounces of melted and cooled chocolate.

Coffee Frosting: Sift 2 tablespoons instant coffee with the sugar, use light cream as liquid.

Lemon Frosting: Use 3 tablespoons fresh lemon juice as liquid and 1 teaspoon grated lemon rind to replace the vanilla.

Orange Frosting: Same as lemon frosting, except with orange.

Maple Frosting: Replace 3 tablespoons liquid and the 1 teaspoon vanilla with an equal measure of maple syrup.

Fresh Strawberry Frosting: Crush enough fresh strawberries to make ¼ cup. Use to replace liquid and vanilla of basic recipe. When available, add ½ teaspoon rose water. A superb frosting.

PRALINE TOPPING

Mix ½ cup brown sugar, 1 cup chopped nuts, ¼ cup melted butter, and 3 tablespoons cream. Place on hot or cooled cake. Broil 3 inches from direct heat for one to 2 minutes or until pale brown.

PINK LEMONADE FROSTING

Whip together in a bowl, with electric mixer, until thick enough to spread, ½ cup frozen lemonade concentrate, plain or pink (do not dilute), 1 lb. icing sugar, 2 egg whites, a pinch of salt. Try this on a one-egg or hot-milk cake.

BAKER'S GLAZE FOR CAKES

Stir together ½ cup water, ⅓ cup corn syrup, and 1 cup sugar. Heat slowly until sugar dissolves. Then boil until a firm ball is formed when dropped in cold water. Brush sparingly on cake while still hot. The cake can be hot or cold. Decorate to taste with cherries, nuts, etc. Glaze decorations.

WHIPPED CREAM FROSTING OR FILLING

Soften 2 teaspoons of unflavored gelatine in 2 tablespoons of cream for 5 minutes. Dissolve over hot water. Cool a few minutes. Whip 2 cups chilled cream until stiff. Add ½ cup sugar gradually, then the gelatine, beating all the while. Beat until mixture stands in peaks. Flavor with ½ teaspoon of vanilla or 1 tablespoon of dry instant coffee. Frost or fill cake. Chill. The gelatine makes the cream stand up for a day.

Cookies

ALMOND MACAROONS

Excellent keepers. Served with a glass of dry sherry, they are truly elegant.

> ½ lb. (1 cup) almond paste
> 1 cup icing sugar
> 3 egg whites
>   pinch salt
> ¼ tsp. almond extract

Preheat oven to 300° F.

Chop the almond paste, add the sugar, and work with the fingers until thoroughly mixed.

Add the egg whites, one at a time, blending well after each addition. Use only enough egg whites to make a soft dough, one that will hold its shape when dropped from a spoon. Add the salt and almond extract.

Force the mixture through a plain round pastry tube or drop by teaspoonfuls, well apart, in rounds on an unglazed paper that has been put on a cookie sheet. Sprinkle top with granulated sugar. Bake about 20 minutes or until golden brown. Remove the sheet of macaroons to a damp cloth, paper-side down, to loosen the cookies for easy removal from the paper. Cool on a wire rack. Yield: about 3 dozen.

NO-COOK CHOCOLATE ALMOND BARS

A delicious, elegant cookie – with no cooking – only the chocolate to melt. They always disappear very quickly.

> ¾ **cup blanched almonds**
> ¼ **cup candied cherries**
> ¼ **cup flaked or shredded coconut**
> 1 **tbsp. soft butter**
> 1½ **tbsp. honey**
> ¼ **tsp. almond extract**
> 4 **oz. (4 squares) sweet or**
> **semi-sweet chocolate**

Chop together until fine the almonds and cherries or, if you prefer, pass together through a food grinder. Add the coconut.

Cream the butter, honey, and almond extract. Add the almond mixture. Mix well and pat into a large rectangle on wax paper. Set on a baking sheet.

Melt the chocolate over hot water and spread on top of the rectangle. Refrigerate until cold. Cut into 2 x 2½-inch bars. Yield: 16 to 18 bars.

CAT TONGUES

The well known French *Langue de Chat*, a dainty, crisp *petit four*. Delicious with ice cream or stewed fruits. Will keep for months in a cool place, in a tightly covered plastic box.

> ¾ **cup shortening**
> ⅔ **cup sugar**
> 2 **eggs**
> ½ **tsp. salt**
> 1 **tsp. vanilla**
> 1½ **cups pastry flour**

Cream the shortening, gradually add the sugar, then the beaten eggs, salt, and vanilla. Fold in the sifted flour.

Drop by teaspoonfuls onto a buttered cookie sheet, shaping like tongues.

Bake in a 375°F. oven until the cookies are lightly browned. Yield: 4 dozen.

CHEW-CHEWS

These are always popular. They keep well frozen, or in a cool place in a well covered metal box or glass jar. Dainty enough to serve at tea time.

> 2 egg whites
> 1 lb. dates, cut fine
> 1 cup walnuts, chopped
> ¾ cup sugar

Beat the egg whites until dry and fold in the dates, walnuts, and sugar.

Drop by small teaspoons onto a greased baking sheet. Bake in a pre-heated 350° F. oven for 10 to 15 minutes or until pale gold. Yield: 2½ dozen.

COCONUT MACAROONS

Another meringue version, as popular as the Chew-Chews. Also useful for using up leftover egg whites.

> ⅔ cup sifted icing sugar
> 2 tsp. cornstarch
> 2 egg whites, stiffly beaten
> ½ tsp. vanilla
> 2 cups shredded coconut

Combine the sugar and cornstarch, and sift it gradually over the beaten egg whites, folding gently. This can be done in the top of double boiler. When mixed, place over boiling water until the mixture forms a crust around sides and bottom of pan, about 5 to 8 minutes. Then fold mixture once or twice. Remove from water and add vanilla and coconut. Drop by teaspoonfuls onto a well greased baking pan. Bake in a preheated 325° F. oven for 8 to 10 minutes, or until golden brown. Yield: 2½ dozen.

LADY FINGERS

The Victorian wine cookie that is used in making so many desserts, such as trifle, charlotte russe, etc.

½ cup sifted pastry flour
⅔ cup sifted icing sugar
⅛ tsp. salt
3 eggs, separated
½ tsp. vanilla

Preheat oven to 350° F.

Sift together three times the flour, half the sugar, and salt.

Beat the egg whites until stiff and gradually beat in the remaining sugar.

Beat the egg yolks until thick and lemon colored, and fold with the vanilla into the egg-white mixture.

Sift the flour mixture, a third at a time, over the eggs and fold in carefully.

Line an ungreased baking sheet with unglazed paper. Press the batter through a pastry bag onto the paper or shape with a spoon into strips about 4 x ¾ inches.

Bake 12 to 15 minutes or until light brown. Remove from paper with a spatula and cool on rack. Yield: about 18 biscuits.

FROSTED MOLASSES SQUARES

These are very old-fashioned cookies which used to be made with left-over coffee; today we can easily make the required amount with instant coffee. When frosted, they look like snow-capped peaks.

½ cup shortening
½ cup sugar
1 egg, beaten
½ cup molasses
⅓ cup strong, hot coffee
1½ cups all-purpose flour
1½ tsp. baking powder
¾ tsp. salt
¼ tsp. baking soda
1 tsp. cinnamon
½ tsp. cloves

Cream together the shortening, sugar, egg, molasses, and coffee.

Stir together the flour, baking powder, salt, baking soda, cinnamon, and cloves. Add to the creamed mixture. Stir until well mixed.

Pour into a well greased and floured 9 x 13-inch pan.

Bake in a preheated 350° F oven for 25 minutes. When cooked, place pan on a cake rack and frost while still hot with the following ivory frosting: Cream together ¼ cup butter or margarine and 2 cups icing sugar. Gradually add 1 to 2 tablespoons hot coffee or, just enough to be smooth enough to spread on cookies. Cool, then cut into squares. Yield: 18 squares.

CRACKLY NUT BARS

Quick and easy to make, these nut bars are chewy with a crackly top. Whenever I make baked apples, these go in the oven at the same time – they are perfect partners.

> ¾ **cup all-purpose flour**
> ¼ **tsp. salt**
> ¼ **tsp. baking soda**
> 2 **cups brown sugar, lightly packed**
> 2 **eggs, unbeaten**
> 1 **cup walnuts, coarsely chopped**

Stir together the flour, salt, and soda. Add the sugar and eggs. Mix, then beat with hand beater or in mixer until fluffy. Add nuts.

Grease an 8 x 8 x 2-inch pan. Pour in the mixture. Bake in a preheated 350°F. oven for 25 to 30 minutes. Cool, cut into bars. Yield: 32 2-inch bars.

CHAPTER 10

CANDIES

MY FIRST FUDGE

Way, way back I made it for my first boyfriend. In those days the cream was really something! Nowadays, I still make this fudge, using whipping cream.

> **3 cups sugar**
> **¼ tsp. salt**
> **3 squares (1 ounce each)**
> **unsweetened chocolate***
> **1 cup cream**
> **2 tbsp. corn syrup**
> **3 tbsp. butter**
> **1 tsp. vanilla**
> **1 cup coarsely chopped walnuts**

Place in a large heavy metal saucepan the sugar, salt, unsweetened chocolate (broken in pieces), cream, and corn syrup. Cook over medium heat, stirring all the time, until the sugar has dissolved. Cover and let it simmer for 3 minutes. This will melt any sugar that may cling to the sides.

Uncover and boil gently, still on medium heat, stirring only a few times until the mixture reaches the soft-ball stage in cold water, or 234° F. on a candy thermometer.

Remove from heat, add the butter and vanilla, but do not stir. Let the fudge cool until the bottom of the pan feels lukewarm to the *palm* of the hand, or 110°F. on the thermometer. For faster results, place the saucepan in a pan of ice-cold water.

Then, start beating the fudge steadily, but not fast. When it loses its shiny look, or if a little fudge dropped from the spoon holds its shape, it is ready. Add the nuts quickly and pour quickly into a buttered 8 x 8 x 2-inch pan, but do not scrape the sides of the pan in which the fudge was cooked, as those scrapings often contain large sugar crystals which can make the fudge grainy. However, do not throw them out, you will always find someone to eat them.

Cover the pan loosely. Refrigerate until cold, which takes about 1½ to 2 hours. Cut and serve.

*To replace the baking chocolate, you can use ½ cup sifted unsweetened cocoa, mixing it into the sugar before adding the other ingredients.

ROCKY ROAD FUDGE

When you just cannot wait for fudge, try this modern quickie with hardly any cooking. For really fast results, chill 20 minutes in freezer, cut, and serve.

**4 chocolate bars, 4½ to 5 ounces
each
3 cups marshmallows, cut in four, or
3 cups miniature marshmallows
¾ cup coarsely chopped walnuts**

Break the chocolate in pieces and melt over very low heat. Butter an 8-inch square cake pan. Measure the marshmallows and walnuts. Stir the melted chocolate until smooth. Remove from heat and stir in the marshmallows and nuts. The candy will then look lumpy, but do not try to make it smooth. Spread in the buttered pan. Refrigerate until firm. Yield: 16 squares.

OLD-FASHIONED VINEGAR CANDY

This economical old-fashioned taffy, with its creamy white color, is still fun to make and nice to eat. If you are too young to have heard of it, try it and see.

**3 cups sugar
1½ cups cider vinegar**

Place the sugar and vinegar in a deep saucepan over low heat and stir constantly until the sugar has dissolved. Cover and simmer for 3 minutes to melt the sugar crystals. Uncover and continue to cook slowly until the syrup reaches the firm-ball stage or 240°F. on the thermometer. Pour into a large buttered platter and let cool until candy can be handled comfortably.

Butter your hands and pull the taffy until it is white and almost firm. Stretch into a rope about 1 inch in diameter, roll into a twist, and snip pieces off with scissors. Place on a buttered dish or wrap each piece in transparent paper.

PEANUT BRITTLE

This peanut brittle can be easily changed into almond rock or walnut brittle by replacing the peanuts with an equal quanity of almonds or walnuts.

> 2 cups sugar
> 1 cup corn syrup
> ½ cup water
> 2 cups peanuts, plain, salted or
>   roasted
> 1 tbsp. butter
> 1 tsp. vanilla
> 2 tsp. baking soda

Place in a cast-iron frying pan the sugar, corn syrup, and water. Cook over low heat until mixture reaches the soft-ball stage or 234°F. on thermometer. Stir in the peanuts and continue to cook until it reaches the hard-crack stage or 300°F. on the thermometer – always cooking over low heat, to prevent the sugar from burning. Remove from heat, add the butter, vanilla, and baking soda. Stir fast and pour into a buttered jelly-roll pan. Let cool for a few minutes, then pull each end to make the brittle as thin as possible. When cold, break into pieces.

CARAMEL FUDGE

This is one of the nicest, creamiest and richest fudges that has been almost forgotten. It was a St. Valentine favorite of the 30's.

> 3 cups sugar
> ⅔ cup cold water
> 1 cup rich cream
> ⅓ tsp. soda
> ¼ cup butter
> ½ tsp. vanilla
> ½ lb. pecans or walnuts

Place in a frying pan, 1 cup of the sugar with the cold water. Stir until the sugar has dissolved, then boil without stirring until the sugar caramelizes to a golden brown color.

In a second, generous-sized saucepan, place the remaining sugar and the cream. Cook over moderate heat, stirring until the sugar has dissolved. Clean the side of the pan, the same way as with other fudge. Then add the golden sugar. Keep cooling, stirring occasionally, until a soft ball is formed in cold water, or 234°F. on the candy thermometer. Then quickly stir in the soda, remove from heat, add the butter, and cool. When lukewarm, add the vanilla and nuts. Beat until creamy.

Quickly pour into a buttered pan. Mark into squares and let it cool.

HONEY CHOCOLATE FUDGE

A delicious creamy fudge. A few grains of soda are added to overcome the acid of the brown sugar which may cause curdling of the cream.

2 cups brown sugar
1 tbsp. corn syrup
⅔ cup cream, light or heavy
pinch of soda
2 tbsp. honey
2½ squares (1 ounce each)
unsweetened chocolate
1 tsp. butter
pinch salt
1 tsp. vanilla
1 cup finely chopped walnuts

Put into a generous-sized saucepan the brown sugar, corn syrup, cream, soda, honey, salt, and chocolate. Heat gently, stirring until the sugar has dissolved. Cover for a few seconds so that the sugar crystals dissolve.

Remove from heat, cool, setting pan on a cake rack. Add butter, vanilla, and walnuts. When cool, beat until creamy and pour into a well buttered pan. Mark into squares before it hardens. Set in a cool place until cold.

UNCOOKED FUDGE

This is the first *bonbon* I ever made as a young girl and now my grand-children are making it. Unsalted butter is best, but margarine is a fair substitute.

½ lb. (1 cup) unsalted butter or
margarine
1 lb. icing sugar
½ cup Dutch cocoa
about 2 tbsp. cream or milk
grated rind of 1 orange

Cream the butter or margarine until soft. Pass the sugar and cocoa together through a sieve, right over the butter. Then mix thoroughly until a thick paste is obtained. When it starts to become too thick to handle, add just a ½ teaspoon of the milk at a time, being careful not to add too much, otherwise the mixture will be too thin. Add the orange rind and knead into a thick paste. Pat into a buttered 8-inch-square cake pan. Spread evenly with a large spatula. Cut into squares. Cover with wax paper. Refrigerate until set and cold.

HOMEMADE TURTLES

Most people love turtles – they make a very nice gift.

½ lb. (8 ounces) semi-sweet
chocolate
½ lb. pecan nuts
1 lb. vanilla cream caramels

Melt the chocolate over hot (not boiling) water in upper part of a double boiler. Keep covered for 25 minutes, then beat until smooth with a wooden spoon. Remove from hot water and let cool to 78°F. on candy thermometer.

Spread the pecans in little bunches on a large flat cookie sheet.

Melt the caramels over very low heat or in a double boiler. Cool slightly and pour a teaspoon of the melted caramel mixture over the pecans. If the caramel spreads too much, it is not sufficiently cooled. After the pecans are coated, refrigerate 30 to 40 minutes.

Then drop turtles into cool melted chocolate and pick up with fingers or fork. Shake off surplus chocolate. Place rounded side up on wax paper. Let stand in a cool room until set.

OLD-FASHIONED MARZIPAN

½ lb. (about 2 cups) icing sugar
2 cans (8 ounces each) almond
   paste
1 tbsp. strong rosewater
   food coloring
8 to 10 whole cloves

Put sugar in a bowl and break in paste. Sprinkle with rosewater. Cut mixture together with pastry blender. When pieces are the size of peas, knead mixture with hands until very smooth and pliable. Cut into 8 pieces. Tint each piece a different color as follows: for apple, use 2 drops yellow coloring; for peach, 1 drop red, 1 drop yellow; for orange, 1 drop red, 10 drops yellow; for lemon, 5 drops yellow; for lime, 1 drop yellow, 1 drop green; for banana, 7 drops yellow; for pear, 1 drop yellow; for strawberry, 10 drops red, 2 drops yellow. Rinse your hands after coloring each piece. Working with one piece at a time, cut each into 6 even pieces. Keep remaining pieces in a plastic bag until ready to use to prevent them from drying out. Shape fruits. To make dimples in strawberries and citrus fruits, roll fruits gently over the smallest teeth in a food grater as soon as fruits are shaped. For apples and pears, insert a whole clove in blossom end. Using plastic leaves, insert a small piece of the stem with attached leaves in apples, pears, and peaches. Put all the fruits on a tray and cover with wax paper. If desired, fruit can be painted with diluted food coloring and a small paint brush. Let fruit stand at least 2 hours before painting.

Store, covered with wax paper, in an airtight container at room temperature. Makes about 1½ lbs.

Note: Marzipan can be divided in 3 equal parts and tinted light green, pink, and yellow. Press each part in a square and arrange in layers. Cut in squares, fingers, or diamonds.

RED APPLES ON A STICK

Children love these.

8 **medium red apples**
8 **wooden skewers**
3 **cups sugar**
½ **cup light corn syrup**
½ **cup water**
1 **drop oil of cinnamon**
1 **tsp. red food coloring**

Wash and dry apples; remove stems. Insert skewer in stem end of each apple. Mix sugar, syrup, and water in a saucepan. Bring to a boil, stirring until sugar has dissolved. Then cook (285°F. on candy thermometer), without stirring, until a small amount of mixture separates in threads that are hard but not brittle when dropped in very cold water. Remove from heat and add flavoring and coloring, stirring only enough to mix. Hold each apple by skewer end and quickly swirl in syrup, tilting pan to cover apple completely. Remove from syrup, allow excess to drip off, then swirl to spread syrup smoothly over apple. Put on lightly buttered baking sheet to cool.

CHAPTER 11

PRESERVES, JAMS, AND JELLIES

BRANDIED CHERRIES

This world famous delight is easy to prepare and will keep 8 to 9 months in perfect condition. Keep in a cool, dark place.

> **2 lbs. sweet cherries, any type**
> **2 cups sugar**
> **2 cups water**
> **brandy**

Do not pit the cherries. The stems can even be left on, only then they are a little more difficult to pack.

Place them in a large bowl and cover with ice cold water. Let them stand for 30 to 40 minutes. Drain, and at this stage only should you remove the stems if you do not wish to leave them on.

Dissolve the sugar in the water, stirring all the time, then bring to a rolling boil. Boil rapidly for 5 minutes. Add the cherries and bring once more to a full rolling boil. Remove from heat, wait until the boiling stops, and repeat this operation twice more, stirring gently with a wooden spoon.

Fill sterilized jars ¾ full of fruit and syrup, place cover loosely on jar, and let stand until cool. Fill each jar with brandy. Stir with a silver spoon. Seal. Turn jars upside down overnight. Then store in a cool dark place, right side up, for at least 3 months before using. Yield: about 4 pints.

DAMSON PLUM PRESERVES

A marvelous recipe that gets all the taste out of this small, tart, and tasty plum. The pits are easily removed once the jam has been cooked.

> **4 to 5 cups Damson plums**
> **2 cups sugar**
> **¼ cup fresh orange juice**
> **the grated peel of 1 orange**
> **¼ cup water**

Stem, wash, and leave the plums whole. Place in a saucepan with the sugar, orange juice, grated rind, and the water. Bring gently to a boil over medium heat, then simmer slowly until a jam-like consistency is reached. Test by putting a teaspoon in a saucer, place in freezer or refrigerator. Only a few seconds are required to see if the jam sets in a sort of light jelly. Then remove from heat at once.

Remove the pits, if you wish. Pour into sterilized glasses. Seal. Keep in a dark, cool place. Yield: 3 8-ounce jam glasses.

THREE-FRUIT PRESERVE

This one is a must on my yearly preserving list. Eating it in the middle of winter is just like bringing summer sunshine to your table. The syrup thickens quite a bit upon standing.

> **2 cups raspberries**
> **2 cups strawberries**
> **2 cups pitted cherries**
> **sugar**
> **½ cup lemon juice**

Clean and mix together the raspberries, strawberries, and cherries and weigh them. Sprinkle them with an equal weight of sugar. Cover and let stand overnight. In the morning, place the fruits in a preserving kettle, add the lemon juice, bring to a boil, stirring most of the time, then cook over high heat until the fruit is clear and tender. This will take from 10 to 18 minutes. Cover and keep in a cool place overnight. In the morning, stir gently and pack into cold jars, sealing with melted paraffin. Yield: 6 to 8 half-pints.

COUNTRY MINCEMEAT

Make it in October for December.

> **1 lb. currants**
> **½ lb. sultana raisins**
> **1 lb. seedless raisins**
> **2 lbs. apples**
> **1 lb. beef suet, finely chopped**
> **1½ lbs. dark brown sugar**
> **½ lb. prunes, stoned and finely**
> **chopped**
> **¼ lb. mixed peel**
> **1 package (4 ounces) citron peel**
> **grated rind of 2 lemons**
> **juice of 3 lemons**
> **1 tsp. almond essence**
> **1 tsp. salt**
> **1 tsp. cinnamon**
> **1 tsp. nutmeg**
> **½ tsp. powdered cloves**
> **½ tsp. powdered ginger**
> **1 cup red wine, brandy or apple**
> **juice**

Clean and prepare all the ingredients. Put lemon juice, lemon rind, and spices in a large bowl. Add prepared fruits, sugar and suet. Mix very thoroughly – the secret of perfect mincemeat is in the blending.

Add liquid of your choice gradually, while blending other ingredients without stopping. Of the different liquids suggested, brandy is definitely the best. Yield: 4 pints.

Place mincemeat in clean sterilized jars. Pour a thick layer of wax on each and seal at once. When stored in a cool dry cupboard, this mincemeat will keep for several months.

Jam Making

General Proportions for Jam
With these basic proportions, you can make your own jam with any fruits you like, in small or large quantities.

Fruit: 1 pound, weighed when prepared.

Sugar: ¾ pound or 1½ cups.

Apples and Other Fruit
Use ¾ pound apples and ¼ pound of other fruit, such as peaches, apricots, raspberries, etc.

When in doubt about pectin and acid content, use part apples, which are strong in both.

How to Proceed
Wash fruits, peel, dice, or leave whole as necessary. Weigh or measure. Place in saucepan, adding just enough water to barely cover the bottom of the saucepan.

Heat slowly over low heat, to avoid burning, for about 15 minutes, crushing fruits if necessary.

Then add the sugar and simmer over low heat for 30 to 40 minutes or until thick. The time varies with different types of fruit. Pour into hot jars, wax, and seal.

APRICOT CONSERVE

Apricots and pineapple are perfect companions.

1 quart chopped apricots
1 cup crushed pineapple
grated rind and juice of 2 oranges
grated rind and juice of 1 lemon
dash of salt
sugar to measure

Combine apricots, pineapple with juice, rinds and juice of oranges and lemon, and salt, in heavy kettle. Cook for 20 minutes, stirring occasionally. Measure pulp and add three-quarters of a cup of sugar for each cup of fruit.

Stir until sugar has dissolved, then cook rapidly until consistency is right for jam, about 20 minutes. Ladle into sterilized jars and seal. Yield: about 3 pints.

CHERRY RASPBERRY CONSERVE

Whole cherries, any type, add flavor and texture to this old-fashioned favorite. Serve it with boiled ham or roasted turkey.

6 cups pitted cherries
2 cups red or black raspberries
2⅔ cups sugar

Pit and measure cherries, place in a saucepan with the raspberries and sugar. Stir until well mixed, then cook over medium heat, until thick, about 20 to 30 minutes. Stir often, as there is no liquid, and this jam must make its own syrup. Pour into sterilized jars. Seal. Yield: 2 pints.

CRANBERRY FRUIT CONSERVE

Perfect to make in the late autumn when fresh cranberries are on hand.

4 cups fresh cranberries
1½ cups water
2½ cups sugar
1 cup seeded raisins, chopped
1 apple, peeled, cored, and
chopped
grated rind and juice of 1 orange
and 1 lemon
1 cup chopped walnuts (optional)

Cook cranberries in water until all the skins pop open, about 10 – 15 minutes. Add the remaining ingredients, except the walnuts. Bring back to boil, boil 15 minutes. Remove from heat, add the walnuts. Pack into hot sterile jars and seal with melted paraffin wax. Yield: 4 8-oz. glasses.

FIG PRESERVE

Try this preserve with cream cheese, or add to it a dash of rum and serve it with ham.

> **1 lb. dried figs**
> **1 tsp. aniseed**
> **2 cups water**
> **1 cup sugar**
> **juice ½ lemon**
> **¾ cup slivered almonds**

Place in a bowl the figs, cut in half or left whole, the aniseed, and water. Cover and soak for 5 to 6 hours. Bring to a boil, add the sugar, then simmer uncovered until the syrup is thick and the figs are tender. Cool. Add the lemon juice. Place the almonds on a baking sheet, brown in a 375°F. oven. Cool and add to the jam. Pour into jars and cover. Yield: 2 pints.

24-HOUR STRAWBERRY JAM

The time involved to make this jam is more than worth it.

> **4 cups large strawberries**
> **5 cups sugar**
> **3 tbsp. lemon juice**

Place 1 cup cleaned strawberries in a saucepan. Sprinkle 1 cup sugar on top. Repeat until all strawberries and sugar are used up. Slowly bring to the boil and simmer for 9 minutes, stirring as little as possible.

Remove from heat, add the lemon juice. Let rest overnight (do not leave in metal pan, except enameled cast iron).

The following day, bring back to the boil over high heat. Simmer again for 9 minutes over low heat. Remove from heat. Remove scum. Cool slightly. Pour into hot sterilized jars. Seal at once. Yield: 6 6-oz. jars.

NO-COOK STRAWBERRY JAM

This jam, with its deep rose color and flavor of freshly picked strawberries, is not one that can be made in large quantities, as it must be refrigerated to keep (4 to 5 months in the fridge or 8 to 10 months in the freezer.)

> **5 cups sugar**
> **3 cups crushed strawberries**
> **1 package powdered or granulated**
> **pectin**
> **1 cup water**

Add sugar to crushed fruits. Mix well. Let stand 20 minutes, stirring occasionally. Dissolve the pectin in cold water, bring to a boil for 1 minute. Add pectin solution to the fruits and sugar and stir for 2 minutes.

Ladle jam into jelly glasses, cover, and let stand on kitchen counter until set or jellied, which may take from 24 to 48 hours. Seal, cover, and keep in refrigerator or freezer. Yield: 6 8-oz. jars.

BLACK CURRANT JAM

This is a super-delicious old English recipe. Do not let the amount of liquid disturb you – a creamy thick texture will develop after a few days of ripening.

1 lb. black currants
2 cups water
1½ lbs. sugar

Weigh currants, de-stalk them and wash. Put in a pan with the water. Boil for 30 minutes. Add sugar, stirring until dissolved, then boil again for 10 minutes or to set point. Pour into jars and cover. Yield: 6 jelly jars.

BLUEBERRY JAM

Do not use large cultivated berries to make this jam, as the small natural blueberries have more flavor. Try them in the winter as a sponge-cake filling, topped with whipped cream.

½ cup powdered fruit pectin
4 tbsp. sugar
2 cups blueberries
1½ cups sugar
4 tbsp. corn syrup
4 tbsp. lemon juice

Place the powdered fruit pectin and the 4 tablespoons of sugar in the bowl of an electric mixer. Stir together with a spoon until well mixed. Add the blueberries. Crush in the sugar, then beat, at low speed, for 7 minutes.

Add the 1½ cups sugar, the corn syrup, and lemon juice. Beat at low speed for 3 more minutes. Pour into freezer container. Cover. Let stand on kitchen counter for 12 hours or until set into a soft jelly. Freeze. Yield: 4 half-pint containers.

MAMAN'S RASPBERRY JAM

This perfect raspberry jam has been failure-proof for 40 years. As soon as the ripe red raspberries appear on the market, I make a few glasses of it as my mother did before me.

4 cups raspberries
1 tbsp. vinegar
4 cups sugar

Place the berries in a sieve and quickly run under cold water. This is important, as they easily absorb water, and too much would spoil the jam. Remove the stems and measure. Place in a large saucepan with the vinegar. Bring to boil, without stirring, over medium heat. Then boil for 5 minutes.

Measure and place the sugar into 3 pie plates. Heat in a 275° F. oven for 20 minutes. Add the hot sugar to the berries, which have boiled for 5 minutes, one plate at a time. Adding the hot sugar this way does not stop the boiling. Then boil for exactly 2 minutes over high heat. Pour into hot sterilized jars. Wax and seal. Yield: 4 to 5 jelly glasses.

GRAPEFRUIT-ROSEMARY JELLY

Serve it with toasted French bread as a dessert or, as a side dish with lamb or roast chicken.

2 lbs. grapefruit (before peeling)
2 large lemons
6 cups water
sugar
water
rosemary

Peel grapefruit and lemons, removing the white pith with the peel. Chop peel and fruit coarsely and put in a pan with the fruit pips and the water. Bring to a fast rolling boil, then simmer uncovered, over low heat for 2 hours. Strain through a bag or a fine sieve.

Measure the juice and pour into a saucepan. Add 1 lb. (2 cups) sugar for each 2 cups of liquid. Stir, over medium heat, until sugar has dissolved, then bring to a fast rolling boil and boil for 5 minutes or until set. Pour into 8-ounce jars. Add ⅛ teaspoon rosemary to each jar. Cover while hot. Yield: 10 to 12 jelly jars.

PORT WINE AND GRAPE JELLY

A must with jugged hare and roast duck.

3 cups sugar
1 box powdered pectin
½ cup bottled grape juice
1½ cups port wine
1 cup water

Measure the sugar into a bowl. Mix the pectin with the juice, port, and water in a saucepan. Stir until pectin has dissolved, then place over high heat and stir until the mixture comes to a full rolling boil.

Add the sugar at once and return to a hard boil. Boil for 1 minute, stirring constantly. Remove from heat, skim off the foam, and pour at once into hot sterile jars. Seal. Yield: 6 to 7 6-oz. glasses.

GRAPEFRUIT WINE JELLY

Unusual and delicious. Superb with roast turkey or baked ham. Also very good with hot toasted muffins or crumpets. A gourmand's treat, ready in 10 minutes.

1 cup fresh grapefruit juice
1 cup port wine
3½ cups sugar
½ bottle (3 ounces) liquid pectin

In a saucepan combine the freshly squeezed strained grapefruit juice, the wine, and sugar. Stir over low heat until the sugar has all dissolved. This will take from 8 to 10 minutes. Remove from heat and stir in the pectin. Skimming is necessary. Pour immediately into hot sterilized jars and seal with paraffin wax. Yield: 5 jelly glasses.

APPLE JELLY

Easy-to-make apple jelly without apples!

1 box powdered fruit pectin
2 cups (1½ pts.) canned apple juice
a few drops red food coloring
3½ cups (1½ lbs.) granulated sugar

Scald five 6-oz. jelly glasses.

In a large saucepan, mix pectin with apple juice and enough red food coloring to tint the mixture a light orange.

Stir over high heat until mixture comes to a hard boil; stir in sugar at once. Bring to a full, rolling boil; boil hard for 1 minute, stirring constantly. Remove from heat.

With metal spoon, skim off foam. Fill glasses. Cool and refrigerate. Yield: 4-5 jelly glasses.

MINT-CURRANT JELLY

Minute-style jelly.

2 tsp. fresh mint leaves, chopped
½ tsp. grated orange rind
1 glass (6 ounces) currant jelly

Place chopped fresh mint, grated orange rind, and currant jelly in a small saucepan. Stir gently over hot water until well blended. Pour jelly back into glass. Cover.

Let stand 24 hours in refrigerator before serving. The same thing can be done with any fragrant herb of your choice and all jams, jellies, or honey.

SEVILLE ORANGE MARMALADE

Smooth, tart, beautiful – perfect for those who like a not-too-sweet marmalade.

8 tangy or bitter Seville oranges
3 medium-sized sweet oranges
2 medium-sized lemons
18 cups water
8 lbs. sugar

Cut the unpeeled oranges and lemons in half, squeeze out the juice. Strain and put the pips in a small cheesecloth bag. Cut the yellow peel and the pulp (not the white part) of the oranges and lemons into fine shreds. Place in an earthenware bowl with the water, juice, and bag of pips. Cover and let soak for 24 hours. Then pour all of it into a large enamel cast-iron pan. Tie the bag of pips to the handle of the saucepan for easy removal and bring to a rolling boil. Boil uncovered until the mixture has reduced by half. This will take 1½ to 2 hours.

Warm up the sugar, remove the bag of pips, and add the sugar, dissolved over medium heat, while stirring constantly. Boil rapidly for about 30 minutes or until the marmalade sets when tested. Skim. Pour into warm dry jars. Seal with paraffin. Yield: 10 16-oz. jars.

THREE-FRUIT MARMALADE

A marmalade that can always be on hand as a gift from your kitchen. You can make it any time of the year.

3 grapefruits
3 oranges
3 lemons
water
sugar

Choose thin skinned, medium-sized fruits and wash. First, quarter each unpeeled fruit, then slice very thinly, saving the pips and the juice.

Measure the fruit and place it in a large non-metal bowl, then add 3 times the quantity of cold water. Add the pips tied in a bag. Let stand for 24 hours. Then squeeze the pips to release any liquid and pectin they contain, and discard.

Place in a large saucepan and boil uncovered, for 2 hours. Again measure quantity in pan as before, and add an equal quantity of warmed-up sugar. Stir over gentle heat until all the sugar has dissolved and boil rapidly until the marmalade sets when tested.

Remove from heat, skim, and let stand for one hour. Stir well to distribute the peel evenly, then pour into warm jars and cover at once. Yield: 8 8-oz. jars.

LIME MARMALADE

To make this unusual and delicious marmalade, requires a span of 3 or 4 days, so take this into account when you begin. The recipe can be done with 2 as well as 24 limes.

limes
cold water
sugar

The first day: Take as many fresh limes as you like and peel off the outer green skin, very thinly. If you have a stripper knife, use it to make thin shreds of the green skin, instead of peeling. Without a stripper knife, slice the rind into long thin shreds with a sharp knife or scissors.

Slice the peeled limes and put them through a meat chopper, removing the seeds.

Measure the rind and the pulp and cover them with 3 times as much cold water. Wrap the pips and add. Let soak overnight.

The second day: Boil the mixture for 15 minutes and let stand again overnight.

The third day: Measure again and place in saucepan. Measure an equal quantity of sugar. Bring to a fast rolling boil. Heat the sugar and add to the juice. Stir until the sugar has dissolved. Then boil until the marmalade sets when tested. Let stand overnight.

The fourth day: Stir the marmalade to distribute the rind evenly. Pour into jars and seal with paraffin.

ICE-WATER SWEET PICKLES

An old standby, which keeps extremely well and can be made in 20 minutes. Add a little to your winter beef stew.

4 cups unpeeled sliced cucumbers
1 large onion, sliced
1 tbsp. mustard seed
1 tsp. celery seed
1 cup vinegar
1 tbsp. salt
1 cup sugar
¼ tsp. curry powder

Place sliced cucumbers in a dish, completely cover with ice cubes, and add water to the top. Let stand for 2 hours. Drain thoroughly and mix with the sliced onions, mustard seeds, and celery seeds. Pack into sterilized jars.

Heat vinegar with the salt, sugar, and curry powder. When boiling, pour over cucumbers. Seal. Keep in a cool, dark place. Yield: 2 pints.

QUICK DILL PICKLES

If you grow your own dill, which is easily done, or if you buy it at the market, you will always enjoy a few jars of homemade dill pickles. They have a very special taste.

4 lbs. of 3 to 4-inch cucumbers
6 tbsp. coarse salt
3 cups white vinegar
3 cups water
7 heads of dill or ½ cup dried dill
seeds
1 tsp. peppercorns
garlic (optional)

Scrub the cucumbers, rinse 3 to 4 times under running cold water. Cut each cucumber in half, lengthwise.

Combine salt, vinegar, and water and bring to a boil.

Pack cucumbers into hot sterilized jars. Place a head of dill in each jar or divide the dried dill seeds, then divide the peppercorns and the garlic among the jars. Pour in the boiling solution to completely cover the cucumbers. Adjust the lids.

Place jars in a deep saucepan, cover with hot (not boiling) water (the water must come right over the jars). Bring to the boil, cover and boil for 10 minutes. Remove jars from water. Set on a tray to cool, then store in a dark, cool place. Yield: 7 pints.

EASY SWEET MUSTARD PICKLE

One of the best mustard pickles, so easy to make and a must on my yearly pickling list. It costs only a fraction of commercially sold pickles.

> 6 lbs. of 5 to 6-inch cucumbers
> ⅔ cup chopped green pepper
> 6 medium-sized onions
> 1½ cups diced celery
> ¼ cup prepared mustard
> 4⅔ cups white vinegar
> ½ cup salt
> 3½ cups sugar
> 2 tbsp. mustard seed
> 1 tsp. turmeric
> ½ tsp. whole cloves

Wash the cucumbers thoroughly. Slice as thinly as possible. Mix in a large bowl the green pepper, onions, and celery. In a large saucepan, blend the prepared mustard with the vinegar. Add the salt, sugar, mustard seed, turmeric, and whole cloves. Mix well and add the vegetables. Cover and slowly bring to the boil, then simmer, while quickly packing them into one hot sterilized jar at a time. Fill jars to overflowing and be sure the vinegar solution completely covers the vegetables in each jar. Seal each jar at once. Yield: 9 pints.

PICKLED CAULIFLOWER

To keep as white as commercial pickled cauliflower, chemical preservatives are needed but the flavor is better without them.

> 2 heads of cauliflower
> coarse salt
> 4 cups white vinegar
> ¼ ounce peppercorns
> ¼ ounce allspice, whole
> ½ stick cinnamon

Separate the cauliflower into flowerets. Spread out on a large platter and sprinkle with coarse salt. Let stand for 2 days.

Add the spices to the vinegar and boil for 15 minutes. Drain the cauliflower, then place it in jars and pour the hot vinegar over it.

Spread a cloth on top of the jars and cool before sealing. Yield: 2 pints.

PICKLED MUSHROOMS

Every year I make two to three dozen jars of pickled mushrooms which I store in a cool room. They will keep for a year and are a great pleasure to eat. Serve them as you would pickles.

1 lb. very fresh button mushrooms
1 medium-sized onion, thinly sliced
1 tsp. salt
½ cup water
¾ cup cider or white wine vinegar
10 peppercorns
8 whole cloves allspice
2 bay leaves

Place in a stainless steel or enamel cast-iron saucepan (do not use aluminum) the whole mushrooms, onion, salt, and water. Cover and simmer over medium low heat 15 to 20 minutes. Add the vinegar, peppercorns, allspice, and bay leaves. Simmer 3 minutes longer. Cool. Divide mushrooms equally into small glass jars. Cover with the hot liquid. Seal tightly. Keep in a cool dark place or refrigerate. Yield: 4 cups.

WHITE AND GREEN RELISH

Each year I double and triple this recipe, as I never seem to have enough. I use it in many ways. In the winter, I love a spoonful added to French dressing or mixed with cream cheese to spread over hot oatmeal bread, where its green and white and red color is most decorative.

4 cups diced celery (no leaves)
1 cup chopped white onions
2 large green peppers, seeded and
  diced
2 large red sweet peppers, seeded
  and diced
2 cups white vinegar
½ cup sugar
1 tsp. salt
1 tsp. dry mustard

Cook celery and onions for 10 minutes in a small amount of water salted with coarse salt. Drain, place in a large saucepan. Add all the other ingredients. Boil until all the vegetables are tender and the texture is good. Seal in hot sterilized jars. Yield: 3 pints.

APPLE CHUTNEY

An interesting spicy winter relish that even improves as it ages. Serve it with turkey, lamb, kidney of all types and, of course, any curried dish.

**2 lbs. cooking apples
3 medium-sized onions
½ cup brown sugar
1 tsp. salt
½ tsp. pickling spices
½ tsp. ground ginger
½ tsp. ground coriander
1 cup cider vinegar
⅔ cup molasses**

Peel and core the apples, chopped fine. Peel and chop the onions. Place both in a saucepan (enamel cast iron is the best type). Add the brown sugar, salt, pickling spices, ginger, coriander, vinegar, and molasses. Stir until thoroughly mixed.

Bring to a boil over medium heat, stirring often. Then, simmer uncovered over low heat for 2 hours, stirring often, or until it reaches a jam consistency. Cool, pour into sterilized jars. Cover. Yield: 3 pints.

NO COOKING CHOW-CHOW

Economical and easy to make, here is a perfect relish with meat loaf, hamburgers, and frankfurters.

**2 large heads of cabbage, cut in
  pieces
6 large onions, peeled
6 green peppers, cleaned of seeds
6 large apples, cored, unpeeled
¾ cup coarse salt
3 quarts white vinegar
3 lbs. light brown sugar
2 tbsp. celery seed
2 tbsp. mustard seed**

Pass through a coarse grinder or vegetable shredder the cabbage, onions, green peppers, and apples. Place in a large bowl (do not use metal) or crock. Add the coarse salt. Mix thoroughly. Cover with a cloth and let stand overnight.

In another bowl, mix together the vinegar, brown sugar, celery seeds, and mustard seeds and also let stand overnight.

In the morning, drain the vegetables and add them to the vinegar mixture. Let stand for 12 hours. Then stir thoroughly and pack into sterilized jars and seal. Yield: 5 quarts.

FINNISH MUSTARD

It improves with age and will keep for months. For an even better flavor, add a little chutney and A-1 sauce.

8 tbsp. dry mustard
3 tbsp. sugar
1 tsp. salt
8 tbsp. boiling water
2 tbsp. cider vinegar

Combine the mustard, sugar, and salt. Mix thoroughly.

In a saucepan, mix the water and vinegar. Stir in the dry ingredients. Stir until well mixed, then cook, stirring over low heat until it becomes a smooth creamy paste. It will thicken only slightly, and will be a bit runny at first but will thicken as it cooks. It takes about 10 to 12 minutes to cook. Pour into small jars. Cover. Yield: ⅔ cup.

INDEX

189